You need not be a runner to find this book inspiring, but you may wind up wanting to put on some running shoes and find God's grace in the wind blowing across your face after reading this book. It is a book that challenges those of us who have moored our boats in the harbor to throw off the lines and trust God for the open seas of Faith and Risk to accomplish something great for Him.

—JHAN MOSKOWITZ
NORTH AMERICAN DIRECTOR, JEWS FOR JESUS

In *Miles to Run Before We Sleep* Tim unloads the wisdom that only comes from completing epic runs like running fifty miles. Both of us have been immensely inspired by Tim's life and writings. Anyone who reads *Miles to Run Before We Sleep* is guaranteed to put the book down a different person than when they picked the book up—just as we are changed from the time we lace up our running shoes till we return home and slide them off.

—RYAN HALL AND SARA HALL
PROFESSIONAL AND WORLD CLASS AMERICAN DISTANCE RUNNERS

We all hope to hear from God, to know His will in our lives. But often we aren't even paying attention or are too afraid of what He might be calling us to do to listen, too afraid of the risks involved. Tim challenges us to listen to God's call to take risks in the face of our uncertainty. To continually challenge ourselves to make our lives about more than just ourselves. After reading this book, it is almost certain you will want to do something to bring hope to others, something bigger than you ever thought possible.

—MICHAEL CHITWOOD
FOUNDER AND NATIONAL DIRECTOR, TEAM WORLD VISION
A DIVISION OF WORLD VISION

People in today's c                  ntic, vulnerable,
deeply personal an               :r than one's life.
Tim's story gets af               ted in scripture
and a persevering                d where fear and
excitement live in t.             journey ahead!

—STEVE SPEAR, CAMPUS PASTOR
WILLOW CREEK COMMUNITY CHURCH/DUPAGE CAMPUS

*Miles to Run Before We Sleep* presents a true and compelling story of how Christ, in His own providential way, compelled one of His servants to adapt to a series of drastic life-altering changes that benefited underserved, underprivileged, and destitute peoples globally! This calling was fulfilled from a position of weakness and led to the loss (or shedding), of health, friends, relationships, security, possessions, positions, and stature; while simultaneously building relationships with, and developing commitment, love, and appreciation to and for people often scorned by society.

It is a devotional guide that will benefit anyone who takes Christ's mission (as found in Luke 4:18–19), seriously. It is very well written, humbly presented, and will guide the reader, step-by-step, to listen for the voice of the Lord in his/her everyday life, encourage them to follow God's Spirit one step at a time, and challenge them to submit to the hand of The Lord in all circumstances—the good, the bad, and the ugly!

I am truly honored to have been involved in this relationship since its inception, and consider this devotional guide to be compulsory reading for all Austin Corinthian Baptist Church (ACBC) members.

—Rev. Philip Hilliard, Senior Pastor
Austin Corinthian Baptist Church, Chicago

# MILES TO RUN
## BEFORE WE SLEEP

### Step-By-Step
### Meditations and Reflections

## TIMOTHY P. HOEKSTRA

CREATION
**HOUSE**

Miles to Run Before We Sleep by Timothy P. Hoekstra
Published by Creation House
A Charisma Media Company
600 Rinehart Road
Lake Mary, Florida 32746
www.charismamedia.com

Unless otherwise noted, all Scripture quotations are from the Holy Bible, New International Version. Copyright © 1973, 1978, 1984, 2010, 2011, International Bible Society. Used by permission.

Scripture quotations marked KJV are from the King James Version of the Bible.

Design Director: Bill Johnson
Cover design by Terry Clifton

Visit the author's website: www.milestorunbeforewesleep.com

Library of Congress Cataloging-in-Publication Data: 2012937900
International Standard Book Number: 978-1-61638-997-0
E-book International Standard Book Number: 978-1-61638-998-7

While the author has made every effort to provide accurate telephone numbers and Internet addresses at the time of publication, neither the publisher nor the author assumes any responsibility for errors or for changes that occur after publication.

First edition

12 13 14 15 16 — 9 8 7 6 5 4 3 2 1
Printed in Canada

# DEDICATION

*To my wife, Laura, who has always "risked" walking with me in my God-sized, risk-taking dreams and visions—and the pain and joy they have brought.*

*To my children and their spouses who lived with me through that crazy "50 mile" day and other times of struggle and celebration.*

*Thanks Leah and John, Jessica, Aaron and Jody (and baby Hoekstra).*

*To all the young and old dreamers, risk-takers, and visionaries who are changing the world—including my church community, SLCC, and the "fellowship of churches."*

*Finally, to God who, in my weakness, has tabernacled on me to involve me in His great stories that I get to live and tell!*

# ACKNOWLEDGMENTS

THE BEST LEARNING experiences I have had always come as a journey with many teaching companions along the way. The experiences related in this book are certainly the result of that kind of journey. In 2006 my wife came to me one day and announced that she felt like she was a goat rather than a sheep when it came to caring for "the least of these" (Jesus's parable about the sheep and goats). She felt that it was time to change that. It was her expression on that day that gave me permission to listen to God in a fresh way. Shortly after her announcement, God stirred in us significant changes in our lives that included downsizing our lifestyle and many other decisions and experiences, some very painful. I want to thank my wife, Laura, for listening to the Spirit move in her heart. Without that the experiences recorded in this book would not have happened.

As those stirrings were beginning, God sent us people to guide us on that journey. One of those was Jhan Moskowitz of Jews for Jesus who was speaking in our church one March Sunday morning. I shared with him about the adventure we were being led on and he immediately told me that I must write down the things that happen because God was going to do some interesting things. Those words came back to me in 2009 after I had finished my fifty-mile run. This book is a result of those words. Thanks, Jhan.

One other person played a significant role in this book coming to be published as it is. Stephanie Rische, an editor by profession, became a friend on this journey. She had overheard someone talking about my writing and asked if she could read it in its initial form. After reading it she wrote me a couple of pages of encouraging comments and suggestions. Not only was she the first "professional" to give me positive feedback about my writing, but she was the one that encouraged me to consider rewriting it into the form of a devotional. Initially, I resisted her suggestions because I was tired of the writing and had no clue of how to do the rewrite. It was a few months later that one day out of the blue the Spirit inspired the rewrite into its present form. Thanks, Stephanie.

I also want to thank a dear friend, Michael Chitwood, the national director of Team World Vision, for always encouraging me to take risks in my running to raise resources for impoverished peoples. Thanks also goes to a small group of churches loosely known as "the fellow-ship" who have encouraged me by their risky lives and their encour-aging words. A special thanks to Rusty for help and encouragement along the way. I am also so grateful for my children and their spouses who have walked with me and encouraged me through all of my risk-taking. Thanks too to Creation House and the staff there for finally giving this book an opportunity to change lives locally and globally. But most of all I give honor to our great God because my life doesn't make sense unless he exists.

# TABLE OF CONTENTS

*The woods are lovely, dark and deep.*
*But I have promises to keep,*
*And miles to go before I sleep.*
—Robert Frost
"Stopping By Woods on a Snowy Evening," 1923

God help us if we are only willing to do what is easy to do. Rather, let us do what God wants done.

—Bob Pierce
World Vision Founder

# FOREWORD

THERE ARE MANY schoolmasters in life and running is one of the best. Running has taught us many, many lessons over the past fifteen years. God has used running to mold each of us and to develop character traits that we will take with us for the remainder of the road of life. With each day that goes by and with every run we go on we continue to grow. We grow physically stronger, mentally sounder, and spiritually more connected to our Creator.

We know we are not alone in experiencing running as a schoolmaster. Every runner we have talked to can share many lessons they have picked up on the road. Whether it is how to overcome the physical challenge of running a marathon or discovering the power of running for someone else, we are all in this race of life together and will continue to grow together. We have learned that one of the ways we grow the most is from learning from other runners. Even though many people may look at our performances in the marathon or on the track and assume we have it all figured out, we really don't see it that way. We are always still picking seasoned runners' minds and learning how to best prepare for a marathon or the next distance race by gleaning from others' experiences. Not only do we learn from others' physical experiences but also from their character. We love meeting so many runners across the country because runners tend to be very developed people, developed in character that is. Anyone who has endured "the trials of miles" has assuredly learned some incredible things about themselves and others along the way.

The first time we met Tim it was obvious to us that he had been running for a while. His soft-spoken and gentle nature surely had been molded from miles and miles of time spent out on the road. The first time we met we went for a run together along the lakefront in Chicago and we instantly bonded with Tim. He was a soul runner, just like us. He was wise beyond his years and we were eager to glean some wisdom from him as we ran.

When we heard about Tim's vision to run fifty miles, on his fiftieth birthday to raise fifty thousand dollars for the poor in Africa we were not surprised. Tim always struck us as a visionary person but not just visionary for himself but to help others. Tim has always been about serving the poor. Through our work with him we have always been inspired by his servant's heart and the love that he has for the poor.

In *Miles to Run Before We Sleep* Tim unloads the wisdom that only comes from completing epic runs like running fifty miles. And both of us have been immensely inspired by Tim's life and writings. Anyone who reads *Miles to Run Before We Sleep* is guaranteed to put the book down a different person than when they picked the book up—just as we are changed from the time we lace up our running shoes till we return home and slide them off.

—RYAN AND SARA HALL
PROFESSIONAL AND WORLD CLASS AMERICAN DISTANCE RUNNERS
FOUNDERS OF THE STEPS FOUNDATION FOR
ENDING GLOBAL POVERTY

# INTRODUCTION

I HAVE LIVED A very blessed life, one that is truly undeserved. I was born as a white male to parents and a family that gave me encouragement, joy, and many privileged opportunities. I did not choose those things. But I have always chosen to take risks in my efforts toward accomplishments. In my younger years this was primarily done in sports that I was involved in. Later in my life those risks started being directed toward my profession and through my faith. Throughout, I was generally "successful" in all that I put my mind and efforts toward. My reputation was solid and growing as I got further into my profession as a minister. I had a blessed marriage and family life. Things were good!

But then in 1998 I was introduced to an African-American pastor and his congregation and things started to change. I had innocently submitted my heart and life along with my church community to be led by and taught by this pastor and his church. At the time I had no idea what that meant or what the consequences would be. He did warn me that "the deal would come down on me" for hanging around black folk.

Eventually that prophetic word bore itself out and the deal came down. As I learned more about black history and their suffering experience and as I challenged my church to spend time at this urban church, tension began to engulf me from inside to out. Some folks at our church simply did not agree with this journey and chose to move on. But even more so, I could no longer live my own life in the same way I had in the past. I suddenly knew too much about racism's ugly history and its current more subtle expressions. I now had faces always before me. Friendships began to develop. And slowly God was positioning me to learn to identify with the marginalized of our city and world. Suddenly "success" was no longer my leading experience. My church was shrinking in numbers and "business as usual" no longer worked for me. It was later that I began to understand more and more that I was being introduced to the "weakness" lifestyle that Paul describes in 2 Corinthians 12.

The heartbeat of this book is about submitting to the learning that comes from living a life of weakness. This weakness is both that of being human and broken and it is a chosen path where one's life does not make sense unless God exists. As this way of life is submitted to and embraced, God brings you to the end of your own power and then begins to "tabernacle" upon you with what is clearly only His power. The result is that you and I begin to live a story that is so distinctly empowered by God that all we do is live into it and tell it to others over and over again—to God's great honor! And this is how great things happen through us that shake and change the world. This is how dreams and visions inspired by God begin to take shape and affect issues of injustice that are disrupting and confusing life locally and globally. I believe this way of weakness could change individual Christians, the church, and eventually the world. People would experience the community of Christians as humble servants whose way of life truly does not make sense unless God exists. Our lives would simply become His story! The question is, are we courageous enough to join Paul in this way of life?

Beyond Paul's teachings in 2 Corinthians 12 I have been guided in my learning through one primary resource—Marva Dawn's book, *Powers, Weakness, and the Tabernacling of God.*[1] I have never seen or read another book quite like it. And I continue to read it over and over because I always want to go back to my own chosen strong life rather than continuing to live in weakness. This book is relatively unknown and I have actually never informed her about how influential this writing continues to be for me. I would highly recommend it for those who want to investigate the "weakness" theme for their own lives and/ or churches.

So, my companions, I invite you to go on this "weakness journey" with me through the pages of these meditations and reflections. Along the way you will be invited to go step by step toward acting on dreams and visions that you have had for perhaps a long time. Most of us have refused to act on these dreams and visions because they are beyond our power and control. They simply seem to be beyond our efforts, energy, and resources. They are risky and they scare us to no end. In other words, we are too weak to get them done. And yet, these dreams and visions are the things that seem to draw out the most passion in our soul. They are the things that could get us up every day. Ultimately, they are the things that draw us toward what it means to be human in a broken world. And while there will likely be difficulty, pain, and challenge to acting on these dreams and visions, the deep satisfaction, life change, and joy could be worth so much more.

A few words to guide you as you read and meditate. Go through this book slowly. Each meditation is intended to be bathed in for at least an entire week. In fact, I wouldn't move on to the next week until I have appropriately soaked in the topic of the current week. Each meditation involves reading a passage in the Bible, some reflections and stories on that theme from my own journey, some journal writing, and one run, walk, or bike ride each week.

If you are unfamiliar with the Bible, I would recommend picking one up that could serve as a guide to understanding it better (New International Version Study Bible with introductions and notes; the Message Bible, which is in a very contemporary form). Concerning the journaling, please pick up a notebook of some kind and keep track of your thoughts and decisions along the way. This will give you some accountability toward seeing something result from these twenty-six weeks.

Finally about the run, walk, or ride, some of you may be training for an event of some kind that involves running or riding. Others of you may not be experienced in any of those activities. Remember, the run, walk, or ride can be as casual or as intense as you would like it to be. It could be that these runs, walks, or rides serve to launch you into a new lifestyle of exercise that you have been wanting for some time as well as being used to shape a lifestyle of acting on dreams and visions of change. But at least be sure that however you make use of the run, walk, or ride that you put yourself in a listening mode. God loves your life and wants to speak to you about who you are and what you can do to be a difference-maker in this world.

May God show you a life that does not make sense unless He exists!

# Author's Note...

**M**ANY DONORS CAME together to not only help get this book published, but also to help the advance purchase of two thousand or more books. Because of their generosity those books are able to be sold and I am able to donate all the money to World Vision clean water well projects in Africa. In our weakness, we have come together to change the world. Their efforts could result in more than twenty thousand dollars toward more clean water in Africa. I also want you to know that all the royalties that I receive from the sale of this book will be donated right back to World Vision and clean water projects. After all, this book is a result of God coming upon me in my weakness, and therefore it really is His story anyway. It is a story to be told and to be given away toward a greater story!

# PART I

## STEP BY STEP: EXPERIENCING IRRESISTIBLE STIRRINGS

*Tell me, what is it you plan to do with
your one wild and precious life?*

—Mary Oliver, "The Summer Day," 1992

# BIBLE MEDITATION: ACTS 2:14–21

**Key Insights: Write a few insights here or in your journal/notebook.**

_____

_____

_____

## Reflect to Hear:

HAVE YOU EVER had a dream of somehow changing something in the world for the good of all or some people, especially people who would be considered "the least of these"? How many times have you had the experience where that vision of change and risk enters your heart and mind only to be broken off by life's immediate responsibilities? Nearly all of us dream about something that could change our life and/or the lives of others. But so often those dreams get lost because we have more "reasonable and necessary" things to give our time to in the next moment, hour, or day. For me those visions and dreams come to me often as "stirrings" deep inside of me. I get a lot of them. In those moments I often feel as though my deepest satisfaction as a human being would come if I acted on those dreams and passions. But reality has a loud voice. Other people have a loud voice. And of course, we often wonder, "Well, how will I make any money doing that?" or, "How will that ever work and what will others think?" And yet, it has always been that the world shifts and changes for the better by people who have just enough courage to act on a dream or passion. Or as I say, "I am afraid just like everybody else, but not afraid enough not to act."

And so, I wonder if you would consider those dreams, visions, and passions again. What if you and I together, in our small way, through our unique gifts, could be used to make a better world—one that is just, and balanced, and moving toward a deep, mysterious peace—what the Bible calls shalom.

**Key Insights: Write a few insights here or in your journal/notebook.**

_____

_____

_____

Run/Walk/Ride to Pray

# BIBLE MEDITATION: PSALM 126

**Key Insights: Write a few insights here or in your journal/notebook.**

_____

_____

_____

## Read to Think:

SOMETHING HAD BEEN stirring in us for quite some time. We had worked to resist it as best we could. But eventually it worked its way into us so deeply that we were nearly forced to open our souls to a season of irresistible change. For the last decade my wife and I had been learning so much about the challenges of poverty and racism in the African-American community and church that God was beginning to call for decision and action.

The story reaches back nearly a dozen years earlier to an event that changed my life and perspective forever. In 1997 our small, white suburban church just outside of Chicago, where I have been serving as a pastor for over twenty years, was mysteriously brought into a relationship with a black, urban church on the west side of the city. A group of men from our church had been praying and seeking for about two years at various gatherings to have our church community become more a part of the Bible's vision of diversity and unity. We were never quite sure how to go about this ourselves. Most of us lived in the suburbs and typically had relationships with folks who were white and much the same as ourselves. But we knew that God had more in mind for us. We knew from some experiences at recent conferences that many of us had attended, and from our own growing yearnings, that there was a great deal of healing needed between people of various racial backgrounds, particularly between those who were white and those who were black. We began to deeply desire the uniting of the church across long-held dividing lines.

Then suddenly through a few relationship connections, a leader in our church met a local black pastor from the west side of Chicago. Eventually I was also introduced to him. He was in his upper sixties at the time and had a great deal of experience with racial tensions and the call to justice throughout his life. He had spent time with Dr. Martin Luther King Jr. and had debated Malcolm X. He had been a leader in a church in Chicago in the early seventies that was on the cutting edge of racial unity, only to see it come apart at the seams as he himself was fired from his position.

As he began to chat with me about the potential of our relationship, he made it clear that he was not interested in a once a year "black history" month relationship. He told me clearly and frankly that I needed to decide to make this a top priority and to be prepared for the "deal to come down on me for hanging around black folk" and leading my church in this direction. He said that eventually people would not be pleased with all they would have to talk about and hear as a result of the relationship. At the time, I had been serving as the pastor of my church for over eight years and knew that change would be challenging. We had already gone through difficult changes in the years prior. But I felt almost forcibly drawn to submit myself and the church to this pastor of Austin Corinthian Baptist Church. I remember hearing myself tell him that I as a leader and our people wanted to be in a relationship of mentoring and learning. We wanted to come to them and learn. We were bringing nothing but ourselves.

It was that offer that I would later discover served to permanently change my life and that of my church. We moved from a life of ignorance and isolation to one of bothersome understanding and knowing. For the next twelve years we would come to build real, authentic relationships with people who had experienced poverty, racism, and oppression throughout their lives. Their pastor, the Rev. Clarence Hilliard, never held back the truth of experience nor the truth of what he understood from his God. It became truth we could no longer ignore. Our church was done living in the false security and isolation of the Chicago suburbs. We now began to see ourselves as a church that desperately needed the urban church in all of its diversity and perspective.

A group of us started meeting for prayer and teaching every Wednesday morning at 6 a.m. in the city at their church location. This was a forty-five-minute drive for me. I was up at 4:50 a.m. to get ready and to travel to this gathering. After each Wednesday prayer time, we would go across the street to Marvin's Soul Food Restaurant and have breakfast. I sat across from Rev. Hilliard for seven years listening, learning, asking blunt and hard questions and getting authentic, direct answers. We also started gathering on the first Saturday of the month with leaders from a number of other churches from the suburbs and city. These meetings too were for straightforward discussion and prayer. Our two churches also gathered the second Sunday evening of each month at our suburban location for dinner and worship. These times were rich and challenging and were used by God to unite us into a deep bond.

In 2005 the Lord took Rev. Hilliard home after a brief battle with cancer. His son, Rev. Phil Hilliard, was eventually elected to be the next senior pastor. Many had doubts as to whether our relationship would continue. Not only has it continued, but there are now four churches that gather regularly throughout the week and weekends in mutual relationship and ministry. We are presently in our fifteenth year of being together. And still today on Wednesdays after our 6 a.m. prayer and teaching time, you can find me seated across from the Rev. Phil Hilliard at Marvin's Soul Food Restaurant, listening and learning.

In the spring of 2006 one of our daughters unexpectedly decided to remain in South Africa for another semester of study and living. We began to wonder if we needed to change our lifestyle so we could afford to visit her if she chose to stay even longer or perhaps live there permanently. At the same time both my wife and I had been reading a challenging book by Shane Claiborne called *The Irresistible Revolution*, a book that challenged both of us to consider how to live lifestyles of compassion and justice for those mired in the never-ending challenges of poverty.[1] This book fell into hearts whose soil had been tilled to the point of readiness. Shane's challenge came to us in the words of Jesus: "Whatever you have done to the least of these, you have done unto me." (See Matthew 25:40.) This statement struck us differently than it ever had before, and it was my wife, Laura, that was moved to more direct action first.

One day as I arrived home from work I could see a thoughtfulness written all over her face. She then announced to me that she would be pursuing changes in her life because she felt, to use the words of Jesus, more like a "goat" that ignored the least of these than a "sheep" that honored and served them. Over the next many months she was trained as a mentor to help immigrants learn English so that they could succeed in living in the North American culture, and she began to volunteer at an after school program near the west side of Chicago—not far from the urban church we had become so close to. Ironically, we also took a brief getaway weekend in a hotel that also happened to be on the western edge of city. As we walked around the community that weekend we both remarked that we just might see ourselves living in this area in the time ahead. It was as if God was readying us for a change we could not even yet anticipate.

Over the next few months we both experienced an ongoing stirring to make a change in our lifestyle. Eventually that stirring led us to make a commitment to God and to one another that we would sell our four bedroom, very comfortable home in the far western suburbs and at the very least move to the western edge of the city of Chicago, an edge near those struggling daily against the monster of poverty and all of its connected effects. The only condition we placed on God was that we wanted to wait until after our daughter's wedding in June of 2007 before we even would put our home on the market.

In the fall of 2006 I began my seventh year as the chaplain at a small Christian college on the south side of Chicago. It was a job that I not only enjoyed and that was going extremely well, but that had also provided steady and consistent finances for my family in a way that I had not previously experienced. As soon as the school year started I began to sense that God was mysteriously inviting me to lay down this job. My immediate response deep in my heart was, "I will if you tell me what I can do next to support my family." The invitation not only remained steady upon me throughout the fall, but it also soon started coming to me as a challenge—one that would also honor the call to move toward "the least of these." I kept this stirring, call, and challenge to myself. God grew quiet...for a time.

**Key Insights: Write a few insights here or in your journal/notebook.**

---

---

---

Run/Walk/Ride to Pray

# BIBLE MEDITATION: LUKE 8:1–15

**Key Insights: Write a few insights here or in your journal/notebook.**

_____

_____

_____

## Run/Walk/Ride to Listen:

WITHOUT SPACE TO really listen to what we have heard, thought, and dreamed about, we will just go on with life as usual. Nothing will change because there are so many voices always clamoring for our attention. Go for a forty-minute run or an hour-long walk or a good, long bike ride today without any goal but to listen to your spirit, heart, and mind speak to you, perhaps considering the voice or thoughts you sense as those of God Himself. Maybe start out by letting go of things that tend to clog up those places, letting go of the day or the night or what is ahead. Be honest with yourself. Identify and name your fears and anxieties about living out your inspired dreams and visions. Quiet yourself to really listen. At first just listen to the creation around you— the rustle of the leaves on the trees, birds that are singing, critters that are sounding, the softness of the snow as you take each step, the smells in the air, the color of the sky, or the movement of the clouds. Eventually allow yourself to increasingly relax and experience peace, perhaps offering your very life and self to God in a submitted, listening posture. What if? How? One step? A small thing with great love?

**Key Insights: Write a few insights here or in your journal/notebook.**

_____

_____

_____

# BIBLE MEDITATION: DANIEL 1

**Key Insights: Write a few insights here or in your journal/notebook.**

_____

_____

_____

## Risk to Live:

WHAT IS IT that you heard on last week's run/walk/bike ride? Did you experience an old dream, vision, or thought that came back to you once again? Did that dream have a risk factor to it? A step of faith into the unseen and unknown? Did you struggle with doubts and fears? But what could be changed in the world, your world, in yourself and others, for the least of these, if you were to act by taking one small step toward that dream or vision? What if you were used by God with your steps of risk to bump into others' steps of risk and suddenly a small movement came alive like the creeks that make rivers and the rivers that make oceans? What if your humble gift and vision offered to God indeed brought hope to at least one person for a better world—or the possibility of thousands being changed without you even knowing it? Don't ignore the stirrings this time. Perhaps, just perhaps, that step is where real living is found. Write down some thoughts right here today so that you don't lose track of these moments of conviction and inspiration.

**Write about your stirrings here or in your journal/notebook.**

_____

_____

_____

Run/Walk/Ride to Pray

# PART II

## STEP BY STEP: THE TIME FOR TALK IS OVER

*We are not travel agents handing out brochures to places we have never visited. We are faith-explorers of a country without borders...*

—Brennan Manning
The Signature of Jesus[1]

# BIBLE MEDITATION: JOSHUA 1

**Key Insights: Write a few insights here or in your journal/notebook.**

_____

_____

_____

## Reflect to Hear:

I AM SOMEONE WHO constantly dreams about places I would like to visit or even live. I love the woods and I love to go camping. During the long winter months here in the Midwest, I find myself dreaming of our next camping trip. I will often look the place up on the Internet or on a map. I will read about it and envision it. But the truth is, I can't ever really tell anyone about those places unless I actually go to them. Nobody is convinced that I was actually in one of those places just by my description of it from what I have read. When I am asked when I was there and reply that I have never been, the credibility of my description takes a hit. I don't want to get travel advice about a trip from someone that has never been to where I am going.

Truthfully, I know more people that dream about where they would like to live or visit than have actually gone on the trip or made the change. And it is also like that when it comes to making changes in who we are as much as it is concerning what we do. My personal goal is to see all these arenas of my life actually come together for once. I want to continue to dream about making a difference in the world. I want to become the person I need to become to make that difference. And I want to take the necessary steps of risk to put all of that into action. After all, aren't those the people that most affect us in our lives? People who are who they say they are and who do what they say they will do in response to their words and character—and dreams and visions? Character, and the words that often accompany it, is proved more by what we do than anything else.

**Key Insights: Write a few insights here or in your journal/notebook.**

_____

_____

_____

Run/Walk/Ride to Pray

# BIBLE MEDITATION: JOSHUA 2

**Key Insights: Write a few insights here or in your journal/notebook.**

_____

_____

_____

## Read to Think:

JANUARY OF 2007 came upon us with its usual push toward new beginnings; only this time, something was different. God's voice not only returned to my heart and spirit with the challenge to resign from my position at the college, but added an additional cruel twist—resign without any assurance of what is next. Finally, I knew that I had to share this with my wife. When I finally found the courage to tell her what I had been sensing with increasing passion she simply replied with firmness, "I think you need to keep listening." And she didn't mean it with a sense of affirmation but with one of "I think you have misunderstood what you have heard."

But the call never stopped through all of January…all of February. I knew that God was placing an irresistible stirring into the depths of my soul. Laura relinquished with fear and anxiety. I resigned with fear and anxiety and sadness at the beginning of March 2007. When asked by my supervisor what I was going to do next beyond serving as the pastor of my church, I simply replied, "I don't know."

While I continued in the week ahead to be afraid of what I didn't know, I had a strong confidence building in me that would not allow that fear to result in an unwillingness to move ahead with all that God had planned. But as the news started to spread I began to observe some people being unsettled about this decision. I particularly began to observe this in some of the leaders and members of our church community. The potential for doubt and discouragement was very high at this early time in the change journey. But some encouragement came from one of the most unlikely sources.

Over a number of years I had increasingly enjoyed a relationship that had developed with Jhan Moskowitz, one of the founders and leaders of the Jews for Jesus organization. Jhan spoke a number of times at the college from which I had just resigned as college chaplain. He was also always willing to speak at the small, unknown church that I was leading. This always surprised me and blessed me. I always thought that there were so many other churches much larger than ours that he could speak at to raise interest in Jews for Jesus. But Jhan would come and speak to our community at Suburban Life and bless us with a great heart and teaching.

When Jhan came to speak in early March, I told him that I wouldn't be asking him to speak at the college any longer. His immediate, light-hearted response was, "Was I that offensive?" I quickly told him that I had just resigned and that my wife and I were making significant changes in our location, lifestyle, and in how we related to the urban churches and the poverty faced by many of them. He looked at me and with great passion and unspoken encouragement and said, "Remember to write everything down. This is going to be very significant." Little did I know that those words would come flooding back to me nearly two years later. The words you are reading are in large part a response to that encouragement from Jhan.

Three weeks later in late March I headed to downtown Chicago on a Sunday morning to run the first running race of the spring, the Shamrock Shuffle. I was joining with many other teammates who had become part of a charity team called Team World Vision, a charity that raised money to support leaders around the world who were seeking to eliminate the causes of poverty and disease, and to care for "the least of these." It was near the start line where many of us gathered for some final words of encouragement before the race. There I "bumped" into an old friend that I had not seen in several years who worked for World Vision. We quickly updated each other on our current personal happenings. And just as we began to part and head to our spots at the starting line, he turned and invited me to call him sometime because there might be a position in the Chicago office of World Vision that would be a good fit for me.

I spent the entire race reflecting within myself and discussing with a friend who was running with me the craziness of this possibility. But deep inside of me I knew that God had moved. The sense I had was so powerful that I knew God had already made a decision about where I was headed next. I waited nearly two weeks before I made the phone call to my friend, feeling a fearful wonder about God's plans that nearly froze me. My job at the college finished in early June 2007. I was hired to work in the Chicago office of World Vision in July as the local leader of church relations.

But God still wasn't finished inviting me into a life of surrender. I have just a few passions in my life and one of them is camping. I have always used camping as a refreshing time away from metro Chicago, where there was quiet, peacefulness, and the activities of nature that often went unheard and unseen in the urban and suburban areas of Chicago. And camping vacations have been such a blessing to our family, especially when our kids were young. Because camping is so inexpensive, we were able to travel to many states throughout the country over the years. We also loved the fact that we were outdoors and away from technology for several days. It always seemed to us that God enveloped us in His creative presence while we were camping.

It nearly made sense then when God started knocking on the door of my heart to give up the symbol of that rest and peace—our camping trailer. Though I had already resigned from my job at the college, God brought back to us again that we had made a commitment to not only sell our house but to downsize our lifestyle. While we weren't sure of all of the implications of that change, we knew that likely we would be getting rid of a lot of "stuff." As the months had moved along toward the day of our daughter's wedding in June of 2007, the day we held out for before we planned to put our house up for sale, we had begun to see a vision for moving into a small apartment-like dwelling rather than a house. This, of course, meant that many of our possessions would not be able to come with us.

Since I had already seen how faithful God was through the time of my resignation from the college, I had become increasingly willing to open my hands toward anything that God wanted to change...except the camping trailer. That was simply a possession that was too dear to me. It represented peace and rest and family memories. He wouldn't possibly ask for that, would He? I had figured that there would be some way that we could store it and continue to use it. After all, we weren't planning to give up camping. But indeed I sensed an invitation to let go of that treasured possession and symbol.

God was gentle. I would pull into our driveway and see the trailer parked alongside our house and I would feel a gentle call to let go, to open my hands. And finally, I distinctly remember the week He mysteriously opened my heart and my hands and He took it. It was time and I knew it. And it was OK. We sold our gas-guzzling SUV that had the power to pull it. We downsized to a smaller four-cylinder vehicle that was kinder at the gas pump and kinder to God's creation. I knew then that the trailer was next. I borrowed someone else's SUV and pulled it to a local trailer dealership and took whatever they were willing to give for it. The simplifying and downsizing had begun.

Our house was next. As we got closer to our deadline with the house, our daughter's wedding day in late June, my wife increasingly sensed that we would never have to put a for sale sign up in front of our house. Something within her offered a quiet assurance that just as we had bought the house directly and quickly from the previous owner, the same thing would happen to us. I listened and accepted her assurance with a mixed sense of trust and doubt.

We then got very busy. Our oldest daughter graduated from college. Our son, the youngest of our children, graduated from high school, while our middle daughter prepared to transfer to an art school in downtown Chicago. Finally, the wedding day arrived. We were blessed with a great outdoor wedding that went off without seemingly even a bug in the air. It was a glorious evening in the low seventies. We were satisfyingly blessed with not only the weather but also with a quality daughter and son-in-law.

As our guests were leaving from a relaxing reception, they began to offer their hugs and final goodbyes to us. One of our guests, a neighbor that didn't live too far from us, embraced my wife. As she offered her final thanks for a great evening, she asked if we were still planning on selling our home. While we had not yet really publicized the fact that we were going to sell our home, word had gotten out that we were considering it. She then said that if we were still going to sell, her daughter and husband might be interested in checking it out. It was sold to that very couple two weeks later. God had waited for our daughter's wedding and sold it as the reception was coming to a close.

But here's the backstory about the house sale. This same couple who purchased our home had inquired about a neighbor's home two houses away a number of months earlier. At that time my wife wondered why we couldn't have them look at our house. But we weren't ready to sell yet. They actually ended up having an accepted offer on our neighbor's house...but the deal eventually fell through. Indeed, they were intended to purchase our home.

We now had five weeks to find our next home, a home that would be much smaller and in a completely new location. Initially we were hoping to purchase a duplex or two-flat with another family from our church community. But because our house sold so quickly we had only five weeks before we faced the need to move on. We looked and searched together but the problem was that their home was not selling. It soon became clear to us that we would have to move out on our own. We eventually landed in a small three-bedroom condominium in an early 1920s building just two miles from the western border of Chicago.

Once again we saw God's hand in our move. The place we purchased was one that I had casually looked at online a year earlier. It was vacant when I first saw it and it had remained vacant until we were ready to make our move. And as additional bonuses, it was only ten minutes from the office of my new job at World Vision, and was within easy walking distance to public transportation for our daughter, who would move with us and begin art school in downtown Chicago.

All of these unique events made it clear that these changes were being led beyond our ability to plan or control. Many times we were amazed by the day in day out happenings that confirmed all that we had been dreaming of and planning toward. And all seemed to be going so well as we blindly trusted God for our needs and His plan.

**Key Insights: Write a few insights here or in your journal/notebook.**

_____

_____

_____

Run/Walk/Ride to Pray

◊ Take A Step ◊

## BIBLE MEDITATION: JOSHUA 3

**Key Insights: Write a few insights here or in your journal/notebook.**

_____

_____

_____

### Run/Walk/Ride to Listen:

THERE IS A discipline to listening. It doesn't come naturally to most of us. And even if we have some quiet time to really listen to ourselves, we often only allow it to last for a matter of moments. Today leave your watch at home. Go out to the street in front of your residence or to a trail in some nearby woods and just start running, walking, or bike riding. Don't make a plan. When you feel like turning, turn. Or just follow the trail.

Use this run or walk or ride to open up space that is not occupied by goals. Run, walk, or ride to listen for that deep, inward call that you often resist. Listen to the call. Listen to what it is that might be a first action to honor that call. Remember, you were created uniquely with your gifts, your personality, your family background, location, and so forth. And the world needs you and your dreams. The "least of these" need you. People near and far suffering under the oppression of poverty and injustice need you. Decide to take some action on that call that may be action that you have heard pressing on your thoughts before. Maybe, just maybe it is your contribution toward change, toward a better world.

**Key Insights: Write a few insights here or in your journal/notebook.**

_____

_____

_____

# BIBLE MEDITATION: JOSHUA 4

**Key Insights: Write a few insights here or in your journal/notebook.**

_____

_____

_____

## Risk to Live:

THE CALL AND decision to act on a call will likely involve risk. Faith and trust in God is risky business. The Bible describes faith as being sure of what you hope for and certain of what you cannot see. That is a great description of risk. But my guess is that you have always wanted to live like that. In fact, you probably know that you were created to live like that. There is nothing quite like living out what you believe. We all do really know that talk is cheap. People are affected by others who act on what they believe. When you and I risk by taking action steps in response to a vision or passion, others are often encouraged and challenged to do the same. But most of all I think people who are and do what they say often stir up hope in others. And soon together we find that we are shifting the world to a better place. Write down a description of the call you are sensing right on this page. And then tell at least one other person about this call today.

**Write about taking a step toward your call here or in your journal/notebook.**

_____

_____

_____

## Run/Walk/Ride to Pray

# PART III

## STEP BY STEP: CHANGE, BROKENNESS, AND WEAKNESS

*When Christ calls a man, he bids him come and die.*

—DIETRICH BONHOEFFER
*THE COST OF DISCIPLESHIP*[1]

# BIBLE MEDITATION: LUKE 9:23–27

**Key Insights: Write a few insights here or in your journal/notebook.**

_____

_____

_____

## Reflect to Hear:

I HAVE OFTEN HEARD my sister say, "I am all for change as long as someone else has to do it." (My sister is actually very brave and continues to make changes as God calls for them.) And really, don't we all think that way? There are some people that love change, but not most. Most of us find a routine, settle in, and live it out. If change comes, it is usually forced upon us. Change is hard. It requires unlearning a way of life or a habit or a viewpoint first before we can ever see the new way or the new thing. And unlearning and letting go are incredibly difficult in the human psyche.

Most of the time when I go through change the unlearning feels like I am breaking. There seems to be no stability. Nothing to anchor yourself to. Or maybe even no anchor. I have a friend who has told me over the years that remodeling buildings is usually much more expensive than starting from scratch. Sometimes it is best to get out the wrecking ball and just bring the whole thing down and start over. That's really what it takes to allow the stirrings of change to turn into reality. We don't immediately become the change we want or see. First we become broken. We get weaker. And this stage feels like it will never end. We often say, "Isn't that enough? Can't I just move on now from here?" God is especially into this method of change. Maybe because He knows us so well, being our Creator.

I have never changed without first having to die to my own self-desired preferences. This is the hardest part. It feels like you are losing your very self. But this downward place, this place of coming to the end of yourself, truly is the place of hope for you and me in this life.

**Key Insights: Write a few insights here or in your journal/notebook.**

_____

_____

_____

Run/Walk/Ride to Pray

# Bible Meditation: Matthew 10

**Key Insights: Write a few insights here or in your journal/notebook.**

_____

_____

_____

### Read to Think:

ANY TIME YOU believe that you are doing something great for God, you are tempted to elevate yourself over and above any other character in the story. Often times when we see mysteriously wonderful things done in the name of God that have powerful, positive effects on people, the temptation is to think that the person of influence is the hero of the day. But when things are done through faith, that faith is only as good as the goodness and greatness of God. When this is properly understood then you and I become the vessels or instruments for a great story about an incredible God.

It didn't take long for my possible temptation toward the "hero syndrome" to collapse. I was stunned to quite quickly discover that not everyone around us was excited about the changes we were making. From family to friends to church community, there were many who began to question not only these changes, but also the leadership I provided to my marriage, family, church, and personal life. For some folks these changes served to give an opening for a season of questioning that appeared to go way beyond the details of the decisions themselves.

Over the next year we watched as many friends and long-time members of our church community made decisions to move to other church communities, sometimes offering difficult criticism that was filled with confusion for us. We had been in most of these relationships for over a decade, walking with these friends through many joys and sorrows. Suddenly nothing in our lives seemed stable or steady. Often it was difficult for me to wade my way through what was happening. For some folks it seemed as if there had been thoughts and feelings percolating from past years but they were often mixed in with tensions over present changes. I couldn't tell if people were struggling with me, themselves, my leadership, the changes we were making, or all of that combined. At times there appeared to be differences of opinion even within some of the families themselves. All of this was then mixed in with a mountain of emotions that my wife and I were working through because of the changes with our own lives and the lives of our children.

My ability to sort through it all was at a near meltdown status. What had started as an exciting call to an adventure of selflessness was turning into a daily nightmare that was alive when I attempted to sleep during the long, dark hours of the night, and when I worked during the equally long daylight hours. The excitement and joy of the mysterious workings of God in caring for us through decisions of risk was fading. Anger, hurt, and a broken spirit began to take over, leading to greater confusion and tension in our lives.

Now we were not only adjusting to a daughter getting married and moving to a different state, and the fact that we had five weeks to search for a new place to live in a new community, but also to the emptiness and doubt that comes along with the loss of relationships. And all of this came at the same time we had to organize our effort to significantly downsize our possessions. Then in the midst of all of that I was to begin a new job that would require a significant amount of training in skills that were not my top strengths. Along with that, I was to travel to several countries in Africa, which carried its own degree of difficult adjustments. And my wife once again questioned why we stayed with the work of the church when it often seemed more difficult than rewarding. We had gone through so many difficult seasons with the church I had led over the past nearly twenty years that we once again felt worn down, burned out and ready to give up the fight toward a better church and a better world. Laura would often say to me that she felt that there was not one person in our lives that would not at some point walk away from us when things got difficult or when I challenged status quo living.

In August of 2007 we found a small three-bedroom condo that had everything we were looking for. It was near various modes of public transportation. It was in a community that was either walkable or accessible by bike. It was close enough to expressways that we could still easily access our work and relationships in the western suburbs, and yet was also right on the edge of the city and surrounded by communities struggling against the risks of urban poverty. And it honored our commitment to significantly downsize our lifestyle. The three bedrooms would work for my wife and myself and two of our adult children that were moving with us. The small basement storage areas would empower us to give away large portions of our personal possessions. And the location ended up being only fifteen minutes from the main office of my new job. We were also very excited to now be only ten minutes away from some urban church communities that reminded us of all that we had been learning for the last twelve years. Yet our hearts were heavy with the ongoing loss of one family after another as they departed from our church community, a community that was as close as family to us.

A growing sense of stress, anxiety, and sometimes near panic started climbing into my life very much like an unwanted houseguest. Shortly after we moved into our new home, I started sleeping less and less. I couldn't seem to stop the onslaught of worries that took over as my bedtime companions. Was I wrong about these decisions? Did I need to own things that some were saying I had done or said to people that were leaving our church or disagreeing with how I was leading? How will all of this affect the financial status of our church community? How...why...when...should I...can I...? Questions, wonders, and doubts overwhelmed me.

During this season about the only rest I seemed to have was out on the road during runs that were preparing me for the 2007 Chicago Marathon. I was so excited to know that this, my third marathon, would be run with one of my daughters and my son at my side. The nearly daily runs seemed like small retreats from all that would attack my thought life day and night. It was on my runs that I was most able to take a thought and let it go up to God for Him to deal with or relieve me from.

Still a growing sense of personal doubt and anxiety was settling into my life. At the same time I was being called upon in my new work with World Vision to lead other church leaders on extensive travel trips to various countries in Africa. My first trip came up quickly and unexpectedly. In October of 2007, I was to travel on my own from Chicago to Amsterdam to Kenya to meet up with a number of other church leaders. We were to receive some preparation training in Nairobi, Kenya for a few days before we all broke up into smaller groups and traveled on to other countries. We were to gain exposure to the development work that was changing the future for many people and their countries with the hopes that new financial support would be gained back in the States.

Initially this trip flowed with thoughts of excitement only to bump into the ongoing anxiety and sense of panic that was growing in my life. The long flights of seven hours to Amsterdam and seven hours to Nairobi only served to strengthen my sleeplessness and anxiety. Upon arriving at our beautiful hotel in Nairobi, I quickly discovered that my sleeplessness was much greater than a time zone adjustment and jet lag. I would awaken after just a couple of hours each night overtaken by anxiety and thoughts about all the changes and challenges of the past several months. Soon those thoughts were joined by homesickness. I was fortunate to have roommates who were very patient with my nightly noise of getting up and wandering the hotel grounds until morning.

My small group of leaders flew on after a few days to Ethiopia. Once there we traveled by car to a remote area that I thought was to be only a few hours beyond Ethiopia's capital city of Addis Ababa. I learned quickly that when you ask an African how far something is, you should always add about three hours. The "three hour" trip grew to six. We were often entertained along the way by new experiences and surroundings—monkeys entertaining us at a stop for tea, and people moving herds of sheep down the middle of the road on which we traveled. But this long trip too was only furthering my anxiety, fear, and homesickness. During the several days in Ethiopia I continued to experience an inability to sleep for more than a few hours a night. While I was wondrously stunned by my African experiences and the people there, I longed for home...and healing that would bring me inner rest once again.

After two weeks and six plane flights, I arrived home to meet the beginning of November 2007 with the hope of a fresh start. But something new entered my life. Shortly after arriving home I began to experience daily challenges with dizziness. It seemed that every time I changed the position of my head, everything would spin for about twenty seconds and then settle. Initially, I thought this was the simple effect of jet lag. But not only did the dizziness continue, it was seeming to get worse. I would particularly experience it when I would attempt to lie down and go to sleep. With each turn of my head to a new sleeping position, I was launched into a spinning sensation that would make me sick to my stomach. Instead of a fresh start, my anxiety built even further. This condition lasted and worsened as the end of the year approached. Twice the condition hit me so hard during the night and day that I was filled with nausea. In order to cope without constant vomiting during these strong attacks, I would have to sit up in a chair and stare straight ahead with hardly an eye movement to be allowed. These severe attacks would last about two to two and a half days.

My wife finally convinced me that I needed to see a doctor about this growing condition. Along the way it had expanded beyond dizziness to hearing and ear issues. I made an appointment with an ear, nose, and throat specialist. Upon my description of the symptoms, the doctor quickly suspected that I might be suffering from the development of Meniere's disease, a disease that affects the inner ear and therefore balance and hearing. I was immediately taken through a series of hearing tests that eventually determined that while I had some minor hearing loss, it was not the typical loss associated with Meniere's disease. The doctor then set me up in a uniquely moving chair that allowed him to manipulate my head and body to various positions. He told me that I was likely suffering from "positional vertigo." The movement he took me through was an attempt to return small "stones" in the ear to their original settled position in a small pocket-like structure. This procedure did not seem to help at the time but served to only make me dizzy again.

When I asked him about the cause of these stones moving out of position, his reply was that it likely came from a combination of things—perhaps the travel, along with stress. He was uncertain when this condition would change or what could help. The last suggestion he had was that I get an MRI done to make certain that there was no unseen growth inside my ear causing the condition. None of this was good news, since I faced an even longer trip to South Africa in a few weeks. Discouragement, anxiety, and an ongoing sense of weakness combined with a lack of control settled in a bit further in my spirit.

I chose to ignore his advice for the MRI, knowing deep down that the positional vertigo was a result of the stress I had been experiencing for nearly nine months. I also spent some time with a uniquely gifted couple who had asked if they could pray with me about the vertigo and my upcoming trip to Africa. After the prayer time, both of them indicated that they had an overwhelming sense that God was allowing the stress in my life to be symbolized by the vertigo. The vertigo, from their perspective, was a symbol of how God was teaching me to allow Him to control my circumstances through all of the changes of the recent months. Their impression in prayer was that when God was ready to allow this time of learning to pass, He would also allow the vertigo to be healed. While I didn't quite experience the same kind of spiritual depths about this as they did, I did believe that this challenge was clearly in the hands of God and in His control.

A few weeks later in January of 2008, I once again left on a trip to South Africa by myself with plans to meet up with another group of leaders upon arrival. This trip was another great challenge in my heart and mind. I feared that the vertigo and sleeplessness would be even greater issues this time. My flight took me seven hours to London where I had an eight-hour layover. I took those hours to travel into the heart of London to see a few sights. As I got off the train and began to walk by myself to various cathedrals and castles, I was again hit with an overwhelming sense of loneliness and weakness. I called Laura and e-mailed others to be in prayer for me. Several hours later I boarded another plane for an eleven-hour flight to Johannesburg, South Africa. On that flight I was given the gift of a fellow passenger seated next to me who was from South Africa. He shared many stories of his adventures playing rugby and entertained me for a few hours before both of us fell asleep.

Overall the flight went quite well. While I was exhausted upon arrival, I was generally given the gift of sleep over the next few days. Once our group went through orientation in South Africa, we were again split into groups to go to various nearby countries to see the work World Vision staff were doing on the ground. My assignment was to travel with a group of around eighteen leaders to an area in northern Mozambique. This would require two flights and several hours of driving. Throughout the travel and days in Mozambique, God graciously seemed to give me quality relationships with fellow leaders and fairly good nights of rest. The positional vertigo remained an issue but seemed to be manageable despite the constant travel through the bush country of Mozambique over several days.

Finally, our group boarded another plane to travel back to Johannesburg. Our first flight landed in the capital city of Mozambique, where we were to stop briefly before boarding again to take a short flight into South Africa. But when we landed in Maputo and deplaned, we watched as our plane disappeared to the hangar. Slowly we came to understand that earlier that day, rioting had broken out in Maputo over transportation costs. We were informed that we would not be flying out any time soon and were warned not to leave the airport. Not many miles beyond the airport we could see flickering in the sky from the fires that were being set by the rioters. We were stranded for what was to be an unknown period in a third world country. It seemed as if we had just become the storyline in a movie about Americans being held hostage in a distant place far from safety and our homeland.

Could all of this really be happening in the midst of my already discouraged, tired, and anxious state? Eventually the only clear sense that we had was that we were not in control of our circumstances. We had to wait. That night our group attempted to sleep on the concrete floors of the airport with little food and no running water. The water supply to the airport had been cut off and the one restaurant closed down. The next morning in the midst of passenger upheaval and confusion we were suddenly told that we had just moments to get on a plane before officials changed their mind. We moved quickly and steadily to check our bags. No one seemed to breathe restfully until we were in the air and it was clear we had crossed the border into South Africa. We had been stranded for about eighteen hours. We were exhausted and hungry, but relieved.

After a few days of recovering and debriefing with the rest of our group in Johannesburg, I started the long journey home—eleven hours up to London and seven hours across the Atlantic to Chicago. As I endured the hours and got closer to Chicago, I noticed a deepening sense in a place inside myself that is hard to describe. It was a sense of being invited to loosen my grip on my own life and be willing to live out of control. It seemed that I was being introduced to a position of weakness that was unfamiliar to me. All through my life I had made decisions and given effort and had been successful. I was gifted and could depend on those gifts to lead me through my life. Now I was being led beyond myself. I couldn't overcome my own anxiety. I couldn't call on sleep to come over me. I couldn't heal my vertigo. I couldn't bring treasured relationships back to my life and church community. I truly was in a dizzying state of learning to live in the brokenness of weakness. God was sending me an invitation through all that was happening to me that was beyond my control. It was an invitation to open my clinched fists that held my own life and to allow Him to lead in a new fashion.

I arrived home at the beginning of February 2008. I was relieved that my trip was behind me and hoped that things would finally settle to a resting place in my life. But nearly upon walking in the door I was hit with nausea and vomiting. This season of weakness and brokenness was not over. It was only a few weeks, however, before I was invited into another change in my life. Over many months I had been in and out of informal conversations with local church leaders from my church's denomination about the growing need to develop and grow younger visionary leaders for some innovative and creative new urban church development. These conversations resulted in the surprise invitation to join a team that was devoted to developing new church communities. My area would be coaching and mentoring young leaders to develop intentional, neighborhood-based communities of relationships that help release justice, mercy, and transformation along with the love of God in fresh ways to a local neighborhood. I knew almost immediately that God was once again inviting me to follow His lead into unknown territory. That June, I finished up my work at World Vision to start a new adventure that had no blueprint. I was again in a position in which I lacked my own ability to control my life and circumstances.

While all of this had developed during the spring of 2008, one final painful relationship challenge entered my life. One of the leaders of my church community that I had worked very closely with on several key urban, diversity initiatives for our church, informed our church's leadership team that he and his wife were moving on to another church community. This was a loss of great proportions not only for our church and for our growing, diverse, multi-church movement that we were a part of, but it was even more so a deep, deep, loss for me personally. This leader had walked closely with me at a very intimate, personal level. I was experiencing the loss of a friend, a co-leader, and a spiritual soul partner. What made it even more difficult was that I saw him on a near weekly basis at a regular urban prayer meeting that both of us attended. God would not allow me to ignore this pain. God would not allow me to control its effects.

As summer came I once again immersed myself in training for the fall 2008 Chicago Marathon. I had been so blessed to run the last two marathons with a new and growing charity team called Team World Vision. Each year I attempted to raise about five thousand dollars to help bring clean water to various countries in Africa. Sponsors would give pledges as I did the hard work of preparing for and running the

Chicago marathon to bring attention to the desperate need to distribute water and hope to the dying people of distant lands. Once again the training runs were used as a cathartic release and rest for my troubled spirit. I continued to battle the positional vertigo but running actually seemed to help me cope with it.

I also noticed that God was inviting me to allow Him to use that summer as a time of quiet and reflection in my life. My new job started slowly, since I was beginning from scratch. Our church was finally settling in toward a new identity after much pain and loss of longtime members. There seemed to be deep work that God wanted to mysteriously cement into my life. There were leaders in my life that wanted to talk through some of the relational changes that I was going through and perhaps even reconcile some of the relationships, but I knew that I needed to be quiet, open, and in a listening mode.

I continued to train for the marathon all summer long. Again, I was excited to learn that both of my daughters would be running with me at this fall's marathon. There were also several other friends and their friends that had decided to run the marathon, some for the very first time. We formed a small team called "the ragamuffins," and worked together to raise nearly $15,000 for clean water in Zambia, Africa. This effort and the training served as places of deep joy and rest in my life. And slowly but steadily through those runs and the quiet, I began to clearly hear God ask me to give up the management of my life that had become such a way of life for me.

This call came gently but firmly. As I listened I heard Him in my own heart and thoughts ask me to let go of all of the people that I had concluded had abandoned me. He asked me to let go of resentment toward them. He asked me to let go of trying to figure it all out. He asked me to let go of my focus on them and their decisions. He asked me to look through new and clarified lenses into the depths of my own life and leadership. One day as I was sitting on the back porch of my home, I heard Him ask me to allow Him to take the past year of change, pain, and brokenness and use it to remake me into who I was created to be. It was an invitation to continue on in the journey of life but with a new vision led from my soul. It was a vision I was incapable of coming up with previously. It was a vision that would continually, nearly daily, lead me to live in the weakness of coming to the end of myself so that my Creator could engulf me and move me toward the abundance of His life, love, and ways. And He made it utterly clear that the past many months had been for me to look at me, and not everyone else.

He had used people, words, actions, loss, change, emotional pain, and physical suffering to lead me toward the emptying of my self-management. It was clear that I was learning about a life path that I had not known before and could not ever introduce to myself. The warm, more laid back days of summer became my classroom of learning. I was beginning to sense that something new and fresh was gradually coming alive to me and in me. This next season of my life would be mysteriously different.

As fall arrived with all its wondrous, color-filled changes, I continued with the final weeks of preparation for the marathon. I was excited! The marathon had become a family event. My wife, kids, and many friends would join together to trek around the course following the runners they were close to. And because of our participation with Team World Vision, the marathon had become even more meaningful, along with receiving the gift of a whole new set of enjoyable relationships. I could now run the marathon and live out some of the call to "act justly, love mercy, and walk humbly with my God" as my teammates and I raised money to be distributed to poverty-stricken countries in Africa.

With three weeks to go, my two daughters joined me on the Chicago lakefront trail with many other marathoners to do our last difficult twenty-mile preparation run. This run went surprisingly well for all three of us. We sensed that this was going to be a great marathon. The following week one of my daughters joined me and many other Team World Vision runners at the lakefront, where we received encouragement and inspiration from Olympic marathoner Ryan Hall and his wife, Sara, both young, successful professional runners seeking to use their gifts to honor God and make a difference in the world. They had recently joined hands with Team World Vision to raise awareness and financial support for global humanitarian work in Africa. It was inspiring to see the quality of their character and to hear their hearts for global needs.

To our surprise, Michael Chitwood, the national director for Team World Vision and a dear friend, invited my daughter and me to join him, Ryan, and Sara on part of a run on the lakefront. My daughter, Jessica, and I were very blessed by a great run and great conversation. Ryan and Sara planned to be with the team on the day of the Chicago

Marathon and it was our privilege to get to know them just a bit before that day. Once again running was playing a key role in releasing joy, confidence, and rest into my life. My inner spirit was beginning to experience new hope and life as I looked ahead to this October event. But all of this was about to change.

The Monday before the Chicago Marathon I woke up and attempted to get out of bed only to discover a severe, nearly crippling pain in my lower back that shot down my right leg and into my foot. The steadiness and sharpness of this pain was like nothing I had ever experienced before. I could not sit or stand or lie down for more than a few seconds before I needed to change to a new position. In fact, I simply couldn't stand or sit still. I had to be constantly moving in order to endure the pain. The pain reached from my lower back all the way to my big toe on my right foot. Immediately, my wife and I began to think that I had a pinched nerve of some kind. She started making phone calls to friends for advice on who I might see who might be able to help with this issue.

Finally, we settled on a nearby chiropractor who specialized in sports oriented injuries. I limped slowly to the car. Laura had to drive. As I sat in the passenger seat, I could barely handle being confined to that small space. I needed to move constantly in order to manage the pain and to keep from passing out. At one point I nearly felt like I was ready to jump out of the car to deal with how severe the pain had become. We arrived at the chiropractor's office, where once again I had trouble staying in one place, groaning as softly as I could until I could be seen. Eventually the doctor called me into an examination room, where he assessed that my sciatic nerve was being pressed on and that was leading to the shooting pain down my leg and into my foot.

As I shared with him my plans to run the marathon in less than a week, he offered to give me therapy nearly every day up to the marathon. He had hopes that I might possibly still be able to run. My hopes were much smaller. I began to prepare myself for one more loss of control in my life. I followed the doctor's instructions for each day—heat and cold alternating on my back and leg, along with some daily exercises. Every day I returned to the doctor for more therapy. And slowly the pain begin to subside, seeming to get better each day. I had hope. The doctor had hope. The day before the marathon I went on a short mile run. My back and leg felt much better but I had very little power in my right foot. I decided that I would simply have to see what would happen the next morning at the start of the marathon.

Sunday morning, October 12, 2008, brought me to the Team World Vision charity tent to prepare for the start of the Chicago Marathon. I was joined by my two daughters, Leah and Jessica, along with other friends from our smaller fundraising team, the ragamuffins. I was hopeful, scared, and filled with anticipation. We made our way to the open start area to join about 36,000 other participants. I truly did not know if I was going to be able to run for any distance.

The horn blew and after about three minutes our area of the thousands of participants surged forward in small incremental steps. After another three minutes we were able to start running, passing over the timing mat at the start line. It didn't take long for me to realize that I still had very little power in my right foot. I endured the first mile, daughters at my side, hoping that the pain would go away and the power would return. Just maybe everything would loosen up after a few miles. But soon the pain began to worsen and the power never showed up. Somewhere into the third mile, it happened. My daughters found their steady pace and I watched as they moved ahead, looking back for me to join them. I could only look at them in pain. They looked back two or three more times and then they were gone. I limped along on one leg and one foot.

I continued to limp along, simply hoping that by some miracle the power would return to my right leg and foot. I found myself slowly getting further and further north of the downtown area on the marathon course. If I stopped I would have to walk back six miles. Out of stubbornness and determination I kept up my one-legged running. Near the seven mile mark, Chris, one of my good friends and teammates, pulled up alongside me. He asked how I was doing. I mumbled a simple, short, "not so good." Chris was running his first marathon. He would later tell me that when he saw "the coach" (his nickname for me) struggling he became concerned about his own ability to finish the marathon. I continued on, deciding that I would try to run the first half of the marathon, which ended up looping back to the downtown start area where my family and friends would be waiting for me.

With each step and mile the pain was getting worse, and because I was largely using only one leg, tiredness and pain began to overtake that leg and foot as well. When I finally dragged myself across the ten mile mark I knew that I could endure another two or three miles in order to get close to the start and finish area and to see my family and friends. At this point I was beginning to think through whether I could perhaps do this for sixteen more miles. As I worked my way through mile eleven, I was greeted by the cheer station set up by Team World Vision and Moody Radio. Team World Vision director Michael Chitwood came alongside me and inquired about how I was doing. I told him that I was hurting quite severely. He asked if I should stop, but I told him that I wanted to at least run to meet my family ahead.

Somewhere in the midst of the twelfth mile I was cheered and greeted by my wife, family, and friends. They could immediately tell by both the time it took me to run the twelve miles and the look on my face that I was in agony. I was still considering going on at that point until I saw my wife, Laura. I knew that she was begging me to stop without ever expressing it in words. I stopped, walked to the side of the street and immediately broke down.

At that moment it was as if the past year and a half of changes, pain, stress, and brokenness swept over me to a culminating point. The last piece of control in my life was being stripped away. Running, training, and the marathon had always been something that stayed with me even when all else seemed to be struggling. But it was as if God was showing me that He was in pursuit of every dynamic of my past approach of managing my own life through control and success. He was asking for me to change from having Him as my co-pilot, a mere appendage to my life, to having Him truly be my Creator, Re-maker, Provider, and Leader. I had hit the bottom of facing myself and having to die to my natural and steady effort to take care of myself. I had wanted to learn what it meant to live as a servant and as one who lived out of brokenness and weakness. I had wanted to have God be seen as the final and ultimate and deeply personal power in my life. But I had never imagined what it would take for Him to bring me to that point.

As I gently and quietly allowed the tears to come, my wife embraced me and assured me that it was the right decision. I then encouraged them to move on to cheer my daughters and others that were further down the course. I watched as this small and valued community of supporters left me and moved on.

I stepped away from the course down a downtown Chicago side street limping and alone. My clenched fists of control had been opened and hung at my side. I walked slowly with that symbolic limp back toward the finish area. Ironically, I arrived there to see some of the top

100 runners finish. I needed to turn in the computer chip given to each person running in order to track their time and place. As I approached the bin to turn in the chip, a volunteer congratulated me and placed a medal around my neck. I didn't have the strength or courage to explain my story. Perhaps this volunteer was serving in an unknown way by placing the medal around my neck as a symbol of God's affirmation that I was arriving at the end of myself for this stage of my life.

I limped over to the Team World Vision charity tent to sit quietly and wait for my daughters to arrive at the finish. It was a long wait but one during which I sensed that God sat down next to me without a word and in the satisfaction that we had arrived at a new place in our relationship. We were there together like two close friends who needed no words to affirm their mutual love. I didn't know what would take place from this day forward, but I did know that I would enter the days ahead with a different understanding about myself and the world around me, an understanding that was settling deeply inside of my being.

**Key Insights: Write a few insights here or in your journal/notebook.**

---

---

---

Run/Walk/Ride to Pray

# BIBLE MEDITATION: JOHN 3:1–21

**Key Insights: Write a few insights here or in your journal/notebook.**

_____

_____

_____

### Run/Walk/Ride to Listen:

ONE OF MY favorite places to do a run in is a cemetery. I have been running through cemeteries at various times for twenty-five years and in nearly every place we have lived. Maybe that sounds a bit morbid to you, but I have actually experienced a mysterious sense of life and peace on my runs through cemeteries. In fact, in preparation for the fifty-mile run that you will read about, I spent many hours running through a local cemetery. I would sometimes even stop and rest and read some of the statements on the tombstones. A few times I took notice of someone visiting the burial place of a loved one.

Go for a run or walk or bike ride today through a local cemetery. And take your time doing so. If it is a small one, consider doing some winding loops on the roads that weave throughout. But be sure to listen as you do. Note the symbolism in a cemetery. The reality is that people die every moment and every day. You and I have a limited life too. But even more so, remember as you run, walk, or bike and listen, that in order for you to become who you were created to be you will have to die to who you are right now in one way or another, even as you live. In order for you to be a person that brings about change for a better world you will have to get outside of yourself, die to self, and allow God to begin to remake you and your vision. You will have to be broken and weak before you discover how He will empower you to become what you could at one time only imagine—to do what at what one time you only imagined doing. And in this becoming you will be and do more than you ever thought. Because when you are weak before God, He comes upon you with greater power. And you become stronger. And the world is shifted by people like you to better, more just, more hopeful places.

**Key Insights: Write a few insights here or in your journal/notebook.**

_____

_____

_____

# BIBLE MEDITATION: PSALM 51

**Key Insights: Write a few insights here or in your journal/notebook.**

_____

_____

_____

## Risk to Live:

THERE IS GREAT risk in allowing yourself to become broken and weak. The risk is all that you will have to go through to get there. The risk is the unknown of all of those changes. You don't know what's on the other side. The risk is in being out of control. The path is unpredictable. The journey is very hard. There is a certain dynamic of sacrifice involved in becoming willing to be changed in order to change the world. But I have continued to discover that in this place of brokenness and weakness is where life, and hope, and adventure, and deep, deep joy are born. It doesn't make sense to me as a human being in my limited state. I can only recommend it now because I have gone from reading about these places of change to actually going on the journey toward them and finally experiencing some of them. And the journey gives you a great story to tell. A story about faith, and risk, and God, and adventure. A story that people actually like to hear about. And because it's your story and God's story, people accept it and are changed by it, and take hope from it. You might even find someone saying to you as I have recently, "You live a very interesting life." To live without risk, is to risk not living. How is God breaking you toward a submitted life of weakness before Him, a life that really is the abundant life that Jesus invited people into? Today write down on this page how God is inviting this brokenness to enter your life. Offer the words you are writing as a prayer, trusting that what He allows and leads is always good, even when it is difficult.

**Write about your own sense of weakness here or in your journal/ notebook.**

_____

_____

_____

Run/Walk/Ride to Pray

# PART IV

## STEP BY STEP: THE BIRTH OF A VISION

*Where there is no vision, the people perish.*

—PROVERBS 29:18, KJV

# BIBLE MEDITATION: NEHEMIAH 1

**Key Insights: Write a few insights here or in your journal/notebook.**

_____

_____

_____

## Reflect to Hear:

VISION IS SO powerful in my life. It truly is what God uses to move me forward toward new adventures. Without vision I grow quite content not only to keep things consistently the same in my life, but I also grow increasingly comfortable with being comfortable. My sight goes no further than the most immediate events and circumstances and people that I can literally see.

I think for most of us it is true that without a captivating vision alive in our hearts and minds and activated in our lives, we die to hope, change, and the passionate use of our gifts. Frankly, we get bored and stale. Without vision I do, in a certain sense, "die." But like all that we have thought about to this point, vision can also be filled with the fear of the unknown. That is why most of us get frozen where we are. We consider the unknown and then stop there out of fear and the desire to remain in control of our lives and circumstances. We really are creatures of comfort. But this fear and frozenness is less secure than we might think. The risks are boredom, lack of energy, lack of motivation, and the end of personal growth. And sometimes these things can get extreme enough to threaten our jobs, our marriages, our faith, our connection to a church community, and our other relationships.

But here is the tricky thing about vision: Is it something that you should stir up in yourself, or is it given to you by something or someone beyond yourself? For me I need to have the confidence that it is not something I am just making up so that I excite myself or motivate myself just for the feeling and without purpose. I need to know if the vision is bigger than me. I look to see if the vision is ultimately a mysterious leading from God that is so deeply in me that I am unable to resist taking action.

**Key Insights: Write a few insights here or in your journal/notebook.**

_____

_____

_____

Run/Walk/Ride to Pray

# BIBLE MEDITATION: NEHEMIAH 2

**Key Insights: Write a few insights here or in your journal/notebook.**

_____

_____

_____

## Read to Think:

OCTOBER CLOSED QUIETLY as I rested in the changes to my life and sought to heal from my running injury. I had ceased all running and exercise at this point. The pain in my foot, the numbness in my big toe, and the vertigo continued to linger over the next days and weeks. A few weeks after the marathon near the end of October, my wife and I left for a much needed time away. We traveled with my sister and her husband for a quiet and restful camping trip near Charleston, South Carolina. One day during this trip we went for a long hike in the nearby woods that lasted nearly two hours. As the hike wore on I began to experience the lessening of strength in my right foot once again. I also noticed that the numbness in and around my big toe remained an issue.

The rest of November 2008 became a time of reflection, rest, relaxation, and quiet. I continued with my work responsibilities for both my church denomination and my local church community. I attempted to run only one time. My wife and I went on an annual weekend away with some close friends. Our tradition was to go on a couple of runs in the hilly terrain of Galena, Illinois, where we relaxed each November for a long weekend. But immediately I was hit again with pain in my foot and the clear understanding that this was to be a season of letting go when it came to running—and perhaps other things as well.

About the middle of November, I woke up on a crisp fall morning anticipating my normal routine. I usually had to rise up slowly from my bed and allow the new upright position of my head to settle in for about thirty seconds of dizziness related to my battle with the positional vertigo. But something was different on this morning. As

I slowly sat upright there was no spinning. My head was clear and my eyesight focused. I turned my head to one side and tilted it. No dizziness. I turned it to the other side and tilted. No dizziness. Could this really be true? Was it finally gone? I was scared to believe it at first. In fact, I didn't tell my wife for several days out of fear that it would come back or that this was just a short blip of healing mixed with false hope. But as the days wore on it seemed clearer and clearer that a change had occurred.

Eventually I shared with Laura that the vertigo seemed to have disappeared. But even more so, I shared with her that I had a mysterious sense that God had symbolically made this change. It became even clearer to me that the October marathon day was truly a certain kind of coming to the end of myself. And now this gift of healing was a symbol of and entry into a new part of my journey—a journey that would continue to move me on to learn how to live in weakness in and of myself. And this new territory of my journey had small glimmers of hope that God would work in my weakness more powerfully than He ever did when I acted out of my own strength. I remembered a quote that I had read some months earlier that said, "God has more need of your weakness than He does your strength." I was beginning to understand what that meant.

As another Thanksgiving Day came upon us, I certainly offered thanks with a new, humble but hopeful perspective. I did not make any new plans to move forward out of my own making, but simply rested in this new hope and healing. I peacefully lived in the present moments. I began to live to "be" while allowing God to determine the "become" through whatever was to come. This way of living started to become very enjoyable and was nearly filled with contentment.

The weeks leading up to Christmas were upon us and I was finally free from a large dynamic of the anxiety, worry, panic, and fear that I had been living with. There was a new deeper, unknown place of rest deep inside of me in a place that is not expressed in words. I was more appreciative of this than ever. The season of Christmas, with all of its special family and friends celebrations, is always one of my favorite times of the year. This year seemed to stand out more than ever. I actually most love being able to offer gifts and love to others during this time of year. And this year more than most others, that heart and spirit was quietly and humbly alive in me.

As the new year approached, I was hopeful that 2009 would be a different year. I was hopeful but with no expectations. Things had really settled down in our lives. We had now been in our new home and community for a year and a half. We felt comfortable and at peace about this place as our home for some time to come. I had found a healthy rhythm in my work coaching and mentoring younger leaders in the urban church setting and continuing as one of the leaders of my suburban church. In fact, our church seemed to be in a restful, unified place. It was as though I had sat down and taken a deep breath with great relief that so much was behind me now. I was finally at rest spiritually, emotionally, and physically. All of January was characterized by that much needed restful foundation.

Laura and I traveled to visit her parents in Florida at the beginning of February. It would be a short visit of four or five days. We had no grand vision of what this time would be like other than being away from winter in Chicago and enjoying where her parents lived for nearly half of the year. We arrived on Super Bowl Sunday and enjoyed a kicked back day of food and football together. The one hope that had come to me before we left was to go for my first run in nearly three months. I looked forward to a gentle, short first run in the warmer weather, one that would be a big test of whether my nerve injury had healed.

Monday morning came and I got up at a reasonable hour to head out into the fifty-degree temperature. I did what I had done so many times, put on the basic running gear—shorts, long sleeved shirt, running socks, and running shoes. The first steps, while familiar, still seemed awkward. As I continued into the first four hundred meters everything seemed to be functioning as it was supposed with the exception of the numb big toe. While that injury leftover was bothersome, it didn't seem to affect my ability to run. In fact, as I ran on I knew with deep clarity that my numb big toe was there for a purpose beyond the result of injury. It was there to remind me of my weakness and God's ongoing empowerment of each day moving forward.

My run that morning was on a loop that bordered the small trailer-like homes of my in-laws and hundreds of other retired folks. It was a loop of about a mile. And because of the unique context of a group of older retirees, one person after another either stared at me with wonder or made a comment that reminded me of what many of them had once been in their earlier lives. These comments, along with several invitations to stop mid-run for a coffee break, entertained me on my maiden run of 2009. As I finished my first mile, I did a quick mental check on how everything felt. All was good. I continued on for two more loops totaling about three miles for this first run in weeks. A gentle and peaceful contentment came upon my inner spirit. I was at the beginning of the next stage of an adventurous journey that I was willing to live one day at a time and one step at a time. I had no plans I was personally pressing concerning running, work, or relationships. I was simply filled with a satisfying peace.

We returned to Chicago after the few days in Florida and I was motivated to continue to run. I continued running only three or four miles about three times a week throughout February. In the first couple of weeks of those runs I mostly experienced thoughts of thanksgiving and joy. But something began to stir in me as the weeks wore on.

Months earlier, before my injury, I had joked with good friends, Michael Chitwood and Lauren Wilgus of Team World Vision, that when I turn fifty I ought to do something crazy, maybe run fifty miles to celebrate. Immediately Michael had responded with his usual passion and childlike enthusiasm that I should for sure do something over the top like that. For me it was an intriguing but fleeting idea. But now, a few weeks back into a running routine, this idea popped into my head out of nowhere. I quickly blew it off and let go of it as a crazy idea that would be impossible, given all that I had been through in the last many months, and considering the injury that I had just gotten over. But each time I went on a run, this idea of running fifty miles to celebrate my fiftieth birthday that was coming March 4 climbed its way into my head and made an increasing effort to touch my soul. I couldn't get rid of the idea. Each time I ran it seemed to come stronger, deeper, and with further vision of what its purpose would be.

These deep stirrings about the fifty-mile run continued to rise on nearly every run I went on. Over and over I would think about doing it as I ran only to work hard at letting it go by the time the run was over. But eventually I just couldn't rid myself of these stirrings that seemed to be given from outside of my own life, but that would touch deeply into my inner depths. Finally, I began to mention pieces of these thoughts to my wife and my kids. Right away my wife's response was a very strong "no way." I could tell immediately that her concern was the physical state of my body. My daughters too had a similar reaction. Their last memory of me running was my hobble through the first thirteen miles of the 2008 Chicago Marathon. I knew it would be hard for them to forget my pained looks and emotions. They also just seemed to be concerned about me doing something this physically demanding at the age of fifty and with a lot of the stress I often went through in my work.

As I finished the last few runs of February, not only did the vision continue to gain ground in my heart and mind, but it also began to take further shape. I knew that this stirring was coming from outside of me. I knew that this vision really came through God's unseen work in my inner spirit. And what I began to see was the vision of not only running fifty miles to celebrate fifty years of life, but also to raise $50,000 for Team World Vision and its clean water projects in Africa. As this vision continued to stir in me, I started experiencing an overwhelming combination of passion, excitement, and fear.

March arrived and the vision was not going away. This became increasingly true as I drew closer to my fiftieth birthday. Without exception the vision grew more passionate with each run. I never tried to think it up. I never tried to get passionate about it. But on every run with nearly no choice the vision visited me with an overwhelming call. Wednesday, March 4, 2009, came as a day of quiet thanksgiving for the fifty years of life that I had undeservedly been given. Many people I knew began to think of themselves through the sober thoughts of being old. Not only did that thought never enter my mind, but even more so just the opposite. I was filled with a deep sense of one who was blessed, and therefore, one who also had a responsibility to honor those blessings. The journey of the past few years was continuing as my teacher and guide. But now, instead of breaking me down, this journey called out to me with a new desire to live with the open hands of acceptance and weakness that would be used by God as my very strength. This was an odd but freeing way of envisioning a way of life.

I was very familiar with a practice that God had called out of the Israelites in the Old Testament of the Bible. This practice was called Jubilee. Every fiftieth year the Israelites were to follow a series of practices that would offer a kind of proclamation of liberty to everyone. These practices would allow them to care for the poor, the indebted, the slaves and the land in such a way that everything returned to its origins, a kind of redistribution and celebration of fifty years of living. This practice ultimately served as the foundation for my own fifty years of life celebration—to run fifty miles and raise $50,000 to celebrate fifty years of undeserved life!

As my fiftieth birthday day entered late afternoon, I decided to head out for a five-mile run to celebrate. My son chose to go with me that day, something that rarely happens between us because he is a biker at heart. As we ran I explained to him the vision. I told him that I couldn't help but think about it every time I ran these days, and particularly today, my fiftieth birthday. He responded not only with great enthusiasm but also with a resounding certainty that I needed to do this. We finished the run and came inside to my wife and middle daughter. Once again the fifty-mile run was introduced into our conversation. Once again both of them resisted the possibility. We debated and finally just let the conversation fade away as if it never really existed.

I continued to run throughout March and I continued to experience the stirring of the vision. I did decide to once again sign up for the 2009 Chicago Marathon that would take place in the coming October. My wife gave no resistance to that decision, quietly hoping that it would satisfy this place in me that dreamed of more. But I knew it would not. At the time I really didn't know how to explain it, but this vision to run fifty miles, raise $50,000, to celebrate fifty years of life was one that I knew was laid upon me rather than chosen by me. Words really cannot be used to explain this sense that I had. Toward the end of March I finally asked my wife to sincerely think and pray about this vision. That's all I asked of her. She was willing but hesitant and scared. It seemed as if she knew what was coming.

Laura and I didn't speak of the fifty-mile run for sometime after that. I wanted to give her the time she needed to truly pray and think and listen. I sincerely wanted her to come to her own conclusion. And I really did need her full support if I was going to honor this vision.

April came with its usual hope of the changing season. All of us in the Chicago area, but especially runners, look forward to the hope of spring. My own running continued to go well. I was regularly running five miles about four times a week. I knew, however, that the time was drawing near for me to make a firm decision about the run. Nothing had changed with how my daughters felt about it either. I finally re-approached the topic with Laura. She was honest and straightforward. She hadn't thought too deeply about it, afraid to do so, and was still against it. But she said that she sensed that I was going to do it anyway and therefore felt like she needed to get behind it. This was hardly the affirming endorsement I had been hoping for. The truth was that she knew me all too well. She knew that when I sensed that something was more of a call than just a personal preference or idea that I would be nearly compelled to do it. I think she knew deep down that this was a call that God had stirred within me and placed upon me.

April 12, 2009 was to be Easter Sunday. Easter is always significant for the community of the Christian church, a Sunday that I looked forward to with great joy and anticipation. It always seemed to arrive with a sense of renewal and hope because of its celebration of Jesus's resurrection, and therefore the hope of our own both now and after our death. This Easter was going to be different for our church community. We had planned to hold our celebration outdoors under a picnic pavilion, first eating a light breakfast together and then celebrating further with songs and recalling the traditional story of the Resurrection.

In my preparation for this gathering I had an overwhelming sense from God that He was showing me that this year's resurrection celebration was to be seen very powerfully as a renewal of my own resurrection. He seemed to stir a deep impression in me that I was moving into a renewal season in my own life and that a symbol of that renewal was the fifty-mile run, $50,000 for Africa, to indeed celebrate fifty years of life that I not only did not deserve but also that I had not created for myself. This renewal event of Easter and the fifty-mile run vision was a symbol of the truth that I was always unable to direct any circumstances of my own life or that of others without the overall power, direction, and graciousness of God. This was clearly symbolized to me in the gift of the resurrection of Jesus Christ. It was this overwhelming sensation that convinced me that I was to go public with the fifty-mile run, $50,000 for Africa, for fifty years of life vision first on Easter morning with my church community. I related this to my wife so that she could begin to prepare herself. I was scared. Going public was significant.

That Easter morning was a beautiful, sunny, but chilly morning. Our church community enjoyed our time of fellowship around a light breakfast and then gathered to sing and offer thanksgiving to God for His gift of Christ. I then spent a few minutes reflecting on how the resurrection of Jesus Christ changes everything. The direction of the lives of those of us who believe in His resurrection should be one of great hope and security in both what we know and what we don't see. I spoke of the ironic, dangerous security of risk because of Jesus's words in Luke 12, "Do not be afraid, little flock, for your Father has been pleased to give you the kingdom" (v. 32).

The next statement of Jesus was about selling all that we had and giving to the poor because what we treasure is centered somewhere else. In other words, we can take risks that don't always make sense and that don't always seem to lead to our own security and safety because of the resurrection movement. I then remember hearing myself say that I was responding to this call with my own risk. I described how I wanted to take a risk that would make a difference in light of the kingdom being His and ours together. And my risk was going to be to run fifty miles on the day of the Chicago Marathon in that coming fall and to raise $50,000 for Kenya and a new runners to kids and adults mentoring program in Chicago in order to celebrate my fifty years of undeserved life.

I really didn't know if there was a response right at that point. I was absorbed in my personal fear of knowing that I had just gone public with this vision. And because I went public it was now a commitment. We closed out our formal time together and then I got the response. Most of the response was positive and filled with excitement. There were plenty of "you're crazy" comments and a few that indicated that folks were inspired. On the other hand, I knew that there were others chatting with my wife asking her how she really felt about all of this. But now there was nothing else to do but to go forward. The word was out. I had gone public. The time had come. Serious training was to begin tomorrow and continue for the next five and a half months.

**Key Insights: Write a few insights here or in your journal/notebook.**

_____

_____

_____

Run/Walk/Ride to Pray

# Bible Meditation: Nehemiah 4

**Key Insights: Write a few insights here or in your journal/notebook.**

_____

_____

_____

## Run/Walk/Ride to Listen:

THERE ARE MANY of us that have a vision about doing something significant but then never see it go further than a thought, because we never go public with a plan that honors the vision. The step of going public to family, friends, or co-workers is a frightening one. If you are anything like me, once you go public you are very committed to pursuing the vision—no matter what. Giving voice to a vision that had remained only a thought becomes the first step of accountability. Now you risk failure or embarrassment (at least in your own mind). After all, people are now going to ask you about the vision you declared. In a sense, they will hold you to it. So, today go for a run or walk or bike ride in your neighborhood or in a place where there will be people around. As you pass by people, use the moments to think of going public with a vision of change. Think of the people you need to tell. Imagine their response. Will they be hesitant with their own doubt in response to your vision? Will they encourage you? Will they tell you in no uncertain words that you are a fool? Use this run, walk, or ride to prepare yourself for going public and then having to follow up with action.

**Key Insights: Write a few insights here or in your journal/notebook.**

_____

_____

_____

# BIBLE MEDITATION: NEHEMIAH 6:1–16

**Key Insights: Write a few insights here or in your journal/notebook.**

_____

_____

_____

## Risk to Live:

NO MATTER WHAT anyone says or thinks, you are important in this world and it is of great importance that you go public with your vision for change. Yes, you are only one person. But thousands of "one persons" become a world-shaking movement that can't be ignored and will have an incredible effect on the world's injustices. Who you are, and who you are becoming, is needed by the people of this world. It could be that you are needed by people immediately around you or by people in a distant location or maybe both. God is ready to oversee the movement of your vision to bring healthy and hopeful change to the people of this world. It is not all up to you. But you do have to take the first step beyond just thinking about your vision in order to join with God and His other called people to bring about this change. The first step is to tell somebody, even if you don't know how this vision will ever get accomplished. Even if you don't yet have the whole plan for its execution worked out. Take a risk and go public. I think you will discover that this adventurous first step is very life-giving. Write down how you will go public with this call and vision. But also write down the possible reactions from people you will tell—both negative and positive reactions. Then hand these reactions symbolically to God and ask Him to give you the power and courage to listen only to how His voice is speaking in you no matter what anybody else says.

**Write about going public with your vision here or in your journal/ notebook.**

_____

_____

_____

**Run/Walk/Ride to Pray**

# PART V

## STEP BY STEP: OVERCOMING DOUBT AND FEAR TAKES A COMMUNITY

*There can be no vulnerability without risk; there can be no community without vulnerability; there can be no peace, and ultimately no life, without community.*

—M. Scott Peck
*The Different Drum*[1]

# BIBLE MEDITATION: EXODUS 2

**Key Insights: Write a few insights here or in your journal/notebook.**

---

---

---

## Reflect to Hear:

WHEN YOU CONSIDER following one of your dreams or visions, especially ones that are potentially big enough to make a shift in the world, you place yourself in an extremely vulnerable position. There are so many unknowns and so many factors out of your control. Other people will likely be watching you and how you are doing in accomplishing the vision you declared publicly. You will face times where you feel alone and are filled with personal doubt. You will face times of darkness and despair where you seem isolated away from everyone else. Often your dream will seem like such a counter-cultural, uphill battle that it will take near desperate perseverance to simply stay with it. You will be afraid. You will struggle. You will want to quit and you will become convinced that it might even be easier to accept the embarrassment of quitting than to keep going into the uncontrolled unknown. It is through all of these emotions and conclusions and temptations that you will most need the gift of community. Vulnerability puts you in the best position to actually be available for others to encourage you. After all, you have nowhere else to turn. You have nothing to offer within yourself. It is the voice of others that you will need. And God will send them to you at just the right times—and He will send them often. This will be His grace to you in the midst of your faith-risk. You were, after all, made for community.

**Key Insights: Write a few insights here or in your journal/notebook.**

---

_____

_____

## Run/Walk/Ride to Pray

# BIBLE MEDITATION: EXODUS 3

**Key Insights: Write a few insights here or in your journal/notebook.**

_____

_____

_____

## Read to Think:

THERE WAS A certain sense of exhilaration when I went public with the plan to run the fifty miles and raise the $50,000. But that sense soon faded with the arrival of Monday morning. Suddenly I faced having to not only develop a plan for the next several months of training but I also faced the rather daunting challenge of having two months to get up to a comfortable fifteen miles as a weekly long run. While it was early enough to avoid going into a panic, I still had to simply get at it with the running. At this point I was running a steady five to six miles about four to five times a week. But that now had to increase by about two miles a week in order to get really comfortable at fifteen miles once a week. And so, I began one step at time, one run at a time.

After much research I had settled on a program that would have me running about five days a week with a gradual build up to back-to-back long runs somewhere during that week. This plan was much more reasonable than some I had seen and was put together by an experienced ultra distance runner. The program would formally begin once I got up to that steady fifteen-mile run somewhere in the middle of June. That would be the earliest in the year and in my annual training that I had gotten up to that kind of mileage.

Because I was at the beginning of my training, the steady fifteen-mile long run didn't seem all that daunting to me. Once I would begin the formal fifty-mile training program, I faced sixteen weeks of steady, consistent, and constant training. I would not be able to let up. I had no room to take time off. I couldn't afford an injury. I couldn't grow weary and take a few days off. I simply had to persevere no matter what. And as I looked ahead to the latter weeks of the training, I knew I would face a near mountain in the days of back-to-back two-hour and three-hour runs that would grow to back-to-back four-hour and five-hour runs for nearly three weeks. The program would then end with a couple of weeks of back-to-back five-hour and six-hour runs.

When I looked at this plan on paper, I remained enthusiastically and healthily scared. But when I thought about this schedule in my head I was terrified. I really did wonder if I could do it. My early doubts centered on the questions about doing this at my age and with my previous physical challenges that had resulted in the lingering numb big toe. I had real doubts strike me concerning whether or not I had misunderstood what I thought came to me as a call from God.

It was about the third week of April 2009 when I began the journey toward my first goal of getting to a comfortable fifteen-mile long run once a week. The first weeks seemed reasonable and doable. I would typically go for three runs a week at around five to six miles each, and then my last run of the week would increase by two miles. By the end of April my long run had hit eight to nine miles.

Slowly during this time I began to release the idea of the fifty-mile run to more and more people. Some of those I informed were my immediate family members. Initially they did not say much, perhaps because they simply did not know what to say. Perhaps they really wanted to tell me how much of a fool they thought I was or maybe they couldn't really put their minds around the idea. I had a tendency to forget that if a person has never done much running, let alone anything beyond a few miles, he or she would have a difficult time relating to the challenge of this idea. They may be able to conclude that it was crazy and a long ways but not what it would take to really get it done from a physical standpoint. Most people envision the 26.2 miles of the marathon being a rather insane distance to consider running. Fifty miles was way beyond most people's comprehension. It was just a rather crazy and silly goal.

Not knowing what many people thought about the plan was often the ground used by my inner emotions and the logic of my mind to create doubt. I did become aware rather quickly that my mom and dad were quite concerned about this plan. Even though many of us in our family had taken on adventures of risk, my mom was never able to get over her anxiety and worry about how the adventure would turn out. There were two key groups, however, that I knew I could count on for support. The first was my church community. They were quite used to me coming to them with challenges and changes. In this case, I sensed they were glad that this was largely my challenge and not theirs—though I was counting on them for emotional support and effort toward raising the $50,000. As I shared more and more of the detail of the vision with them, they definitely encouraged me with words and prayers.

The second key support group was made up of close friends who were also a part of my church community, but seemed to have an even stronger sense of getting behind this effort. This group of friends was made up of fellow church staff members and their spouses, a smaller community from my church that my wife and I were members of that gathered every other Friday for a meal and time of encouragement, and some of our closest friends within those smaller groups. This group of very close friends, made up primarily of my sister and her husband and another family that we spent a lot of time with, saw this vision as one filled with dynamic excitement and adventure. One friend in particular seemed excited to see someone like me taking on something of a near super-human effort. Throughout my time of preparation it was these relationships that most kept me going in the face of personal doubt and the growing sense I had that there was a certain "foolishness" to this whole vision.

As May arrived, I continued to increase my weekly long run by nearly two miles a week, and by mid-May I was up to a comfortable ten to eleven miles for my once-a-week long run. Even though I was only about a month into my commitment since going public, I was beginning to sense how much I would need encouragement along the way. The challenge of never being able to ease up for any one week was emotionally and physically taxing. Perhaps the hardest part of the discipline of each week was the planning that it took to figure out where to place each increasingly longer run. I could never quite keep the plan consistent due to the nature of my work schedule. Each week was unique and took hard work to do the well thought out schedule planning.

As the month marched on I set up a time for Team World Vision national director, Michael Chitwood, to come and speak at our Sunday morning church gathering. I was concerned that unless there was a different voice speaking about the fifty-mile run, it would be easy for people to forget about it since it seemed many months off to many of them. Michael did a great job speaking that Sunday morning. He primarily spent time helping our church community understand the ongoing great need for clean water in Kenya and also for the running mentoring club for at-risk kids and adults that both of us had envisioned for a number of years. He also issued a challenge for them to really engage support for me as I continued with my vision. After our gathering finished, a young woman that I knew well came up to speak with me. She had been taking a high school student who participated in a ministry that she led with her to our gatherings. Both of them had a joyous seriousness written across their faces. Annette then told me that she and Maddie wanted to run the marathon portion of the fifty-mile run with me and that this was primarily Maddie the high school student's idea. They also were clear that they would be committed to raising at least $2,000 together toward the $50,000. After making sure that they understood that the marathon part of the run could be very slow and difficult for me, I told them how very encouraged and excited I was to have them on the team.

As I drove away from our church gathering later that afternoon, I had two rising emotions come upon me—I felt encouraged and excited, but almost at the same time I was exhausted and overwhelmed by the work ahead that was required by this vision. And it seemed that the further I got away from that very encouraging time with my church community, the more down I got. I really couldn't understand why those feelings of despair were so powerful. And in the midst of the despair, a strong, monstrous sense of doubt started attacking me with a fierce, dark voice. By the time I got home I was ready to simply sleep and sit all afternoon. The only thing that overcame that desire was a decision to once again get myself out on the streets for another six-to-seven mile run—a distance that was now commonplace in my weekly schedule of runs.

As I launched out on one of my usual paths for that distance, the dark despair brought an immediate tiredness to my physical being. Every step felt heavy, almost as if I were running this distance for the first time after weeks of no running. But, as every runner knows, there will be days like this and you have to simply run through them.

After about three miles, I approached my turn around point. I made a left hand turn north up a busy street in order to reach the street by which I would return. But immediately upon making the northern turn I heard a voice call out to me, "Hey, do you know anything about

World Vision?" I then remembered that I chose to wear my World Vision running shirt that day, as I often did, so that maybe someone would notice it and possibly strike up a conversation. I quickly stopped and turned to one side and noticed an African-American woman waiting for me. I turned off my watch timer and indicated that I knew quite a bit about the nonprofit organization World Vision. We then launched into a ten-minute conversation in which she told me that she had heard via a program on Moody radio about the idea that people could run the Chicago Marathon for Team World Vision in order to raise money for Africa. I enthusiastically affirmed what she had heard and explained more about how it all worked.

As she and I parted ways, both of us were excited about our encounter. And this was exactly what I needed on that day to work my way through my despair and weariness. God had sent another person, another voice, and a sense that I was not alone on my journey. That run continued the theme of the morning about the need for "community" in order to see this vision through. It wasn't until later that night that I truly understood the battle of that day. While I had continued to be strongly committed to the vision I sensed God had given to me, there would always be a battle within me that sought to bring isolation and loneliness, as if someone wanted me to feel defeat in this upstream swim. I would need God's wisdom and power given in all kinds of ways, but especially through "community," in order to stay the course toward the 50/50 vision.

By mid-June, I had finally worked my way up to a fifteen-mile long run. I was not comfortable at this distance, however. And I also faced a several day break in order to travel out to California to visit my brother and his family. It was always difficult to maintain a running routine while away. I managed to get a few short runs of four to five miles in while I was there but nothing close to maintaining my seven- to eight-mile regular runs, nor my once-a-week fifteen-mile run.

Once we returned from that trip, I pushed myself to quickly return to the regular routine, including the fifteen-mile run. It was then finally time to begin the sixteen-week formal training program (see below). It generally worked best for me to take my rest days on Sundays and Wednesdays. I would do the back-to-back long runs on Mondays and Tuesdays (the two runs listed at the end of each week). Thursdays, Fridays, and Saturdays were used for doing the other runs you see listed. I had made the decision by then as well, about my pace for the fifty-mile run. I had decided to run eleven-minute miles, running eleven minutes and walking one minute, putting me at about five miles an hour. Everything I had read indicated that I could figure out my potential time for the fifty-mile run by taking my best marathon time (four hours and five minutes), doubling it, and adding two more hours. That would put me at approximately ten hours for the fifty-mile run.

## MY 16-WEEK TRAINING CHALLENGE:

### Key:

(MP) Marathon Pace: the pace/effort you can hold in a marathon

(HMP) Half-Marathon Pace: the per-mile average of your best half-marathon

(TMP) 10-Mile Pace: the per-mile pace of your fastest 10-miler

Recovery for HMP/TMP: Jog slowly until you feel fresh enough to start the next repetition.

**Week 1**
Rest
6–10 miles, including 4x1 mile at TMP
Easy 5-mile jog
7–9 miles, middle 3 at MP
Rest
90-minute run
3-hour run (or about 18 miles)

**Week 2**
Rest
6–10 Miles, including 4x1 mile at TMP
Easy 5-mile jog
7–9 miles, middle 3 at MP
Rest
90-minute run
3-hour run

**Week 3**
Rest
6–10 miles, including 2x2 miles at HMP
Easy 5-mile jog
7–9 miles, middle 3 at MP (5:00)
Rest
2-hour run
3.5-hour run (or about 20 miles)

**Week 4**
Rest
5–8 miles, including 3x1 mile at TMP
Easy 5-mile jog
6 miles, middle 2 at MP
Rest
1.5-hour run
2-hour run

**Week 5**
Rest
9 miles, including 6x1 mile at TMP
Easy 5-mile jog
9 miles, middle 3 at MP
Rest
3.5- to 4-hour run (or about 20–24 miles)
3-hour run

**Week 6**
Rest
9 miles, including 6x1 mile at TMP
Easy 5-mile jog
9 miles, middle 3 at MP
Rest
3.5- to 4-hour run
3-hour run

**Week 7**
Rest
9 miles, including 6x1 mile at HMP
Easy 5-mile jog
9 miles, middle 3 at MP
Rest
3.5- to 4-hour run
3-hour run, last hour at MP

**Week 8**
Rest
9 miles, including 3x2 miles at HMP
Easy 5-mile jog
9 miles, middle 3 at MP
Rest
2-hour run
2.5-hour run

**Week 9**
Rest
9 miles, including 6x1 miles at TMP
Easy 5-mile jog
9 miles, middle 3 at MP
Rest
4-hour run
3.5-hour run, last hour at MP

**Week 10**
Rest
9 miles, including 6x1 miles at TMP
Easy 5-mile jog
9 miles, middle 3 at MP
Rest
4-hour run
3.5-hour run, last hour at MP

**Week 11**
Rest
9 miles, including 3x2 miles at HMP
Easy 5-mile jog
9 miles, middle 3 at MP
Rest
2.5-hour run
3-hour run

**Week 12**
Rest
9 miles, including 6x1 mile at TMP
Easy 5-mile jog
9 miles, middle 3 at MP
Rest
4-hour run
5-hour run (or about 27–29 miles)

**Week 13**
Rest
9 miles, including 6x1 mile at TMP
Easy 5-mile jog
9 miles, middle 3 at MP
Rest
4-hour run
5-hour run

**Week 14**
Rest
9 miles, including 4x1 mile at TMP
Easy 5-mile jog
9 miles, middle 3 at MP
Rest
2-hour run
2-hour run

**Week 15**
Rest
7 miles, including 3x1 mile at MP
Easy 5-mile jog
7 miles, middle 3 at MP
Rest
1.5-hour run
Easy 1-hour jog

**Week 16**
Rest
6 miles, middle 3 at HMP
Easy 5-mile jog
Easy 3-mile jog
Rest: Stay off your feet
50-mile race
Rest. (Duh.)

One of the real challenges that I faced in the ongoing training was having to run on more urban roads. This meant traffic, and traffic meant time and risk when it came to running. We live in an area that is right on the western edge of the city of Chicago and is much more city-like than suburb-like. Things are compact and there is a significant population in just a few square miles. I faced doing most of my running on city streets through neighborhoods filled with houses and people. There was no convenient trail in the woods that I could access. And due to the amount of time it took to do the runs, I didn't have the time to travel to a more open area where there might be trails away from traffic and stoplights. My routine typically became getting up early to begin my work day and get my meetings done so that by 2:30 in the afternoon I could be out on the road to run. Of course there would eventually be times where I would have to devote a good part of the day to four- and five-hour or longer runs.

A great discovery that I made when we moved to our neighborhood was the Concordia Cemetery. This became a great place to do many of the miles of a particular run. It was obviously quiet. There were very few cars and no stoplights. The outer road of the cemetery was about two miles in its entirety. And if I wanted to I could weave up and down many other rows of roads between the many grave markers. The runs I did in the cemetery became one of the great gifts of the summer. It was as if I were on a quiet retreat without any disruptions.

The cemetery also became a significant symbol to me as I moved through the steps of the fifty-mile vision. No one can control when they will live or die. I had little control over how the fifty-mile, $50,000 vision would work or get accomplished. In order to accomplish this great challenge, I needed to constantly surrender myself to God in a position of vulnerable weakness. The cemetery gave me a visible symbol of my inability to control this vision or to ultimately accomplish it outside of God's gracious empowerment. In the midst of all the lives that had been sown back to the ground, I saw how every day of life was a gift and every breath and step of my running was a gift.

Often I spent two hours or ten miles running through these symbolic surroundings before I moved on to other running locations. Over the weeks of running through the cemetery the maintenance workers and some of the managers became familiar faces. While initially they would make sure to tell me when they were closing the front gates, eventually they just let me do my thing and exit out one of the back gates. Finally, one day I was called over by one of the managers who inquired about my constant running through the cemetery. I was able to share the story of the fifty-mile run with him. He was very encouraging but then continued with a warning to be careful. Apparently, the week before, a couple who was visiting a grave site was held up at gunpoint in the middle of the afternoon.

By this time I had also started the fundraising for the $50,000 for the Kenya clean water projects and the start up of the local running/ walking mentoring club for students and adults in impoverished and at-risk communities. Fundraising is always an interesting challenge. My experience to date was that most people would not give early on but would wait until much closer to the fifty-mile run. Yet I still needed to keep people with me on the journey and start inviting them to give immediately. Perhaps the hardest part of the fundraising was getting enough early success so that I would have a sense that I was on the right path and that God was in it with me. Again, these were things that I couldn't really control. I could ask and invite. People had to decide whether to participate. And in my mind, God had to move on their hearts with conviction that this vision was of great, world-shaking importance.

There were several really encouraging early gifts and commitments that were significant in affirming my vision. I have had the great joy of getting to know a new personal barber in our new neighborhood. Rita is unique in being a woman working in a "traditional" barbershop. What I love about Rita is her energetic and outgoing personality. She is easy to get to know and easy to talk to while I get my hair cut. So naturally I shared this crazy vision with her quite early on. Immediately she said that she would commit to a donation. I knew she would follow through since I would be seeing her about every five or six weeks leading toward the run.

What I wasn't aware of the day I shared with her was that Joe, the owner of the barbershop, was off in a corner waiting for his next appointment and overheard our conversation about the run. As I was ready to leave, Joe got up and walked over and told me he had heard my description of the run and fundraising. He shared how touched he was by my willingness to take this commitment on and then he handed me cash on the spot. I was rather shocked. He didn't really know me. He didn't really know if he could trust that I would truly get the cash to the project. And yet he gave. I left incredibly encouraged.

Another early gift came from a person that I see at least a few times a week at my local Panera Bread cafe. We happen to live directly across the street from this Panera Bread and so I start my mornings there at 7 a.m. about three days a week. When you do something like that consistently you usually begin to see the same people on a regular basis. I have had the privilege of getting to know some of the Panera staff: Pete, Gwen, and several others. I have also gotten to know some of the other customers. One of those is Ron.

Ron and I greeted each other on those mornings for several months until finally I had to introduce myself. Somehow Ron and I got into further conversation about what I did for a living. When Ron found out that I was a minister, it seemed like he had immediate respect for me. I later found out that Ron was a devout, practicing Catholic who loved God. From that moment on he would often encourage me with a sentence or two about how he knew my work was important and well done. Once I shared with Ron what I was doing with the run, he responded the next week with a check for a contribution.

Again, I was encouraged by people I didn't know well, but who were placed in my path with purpose. And there were many others who gave or committed in the early months in surprising ways. Anthony and Kim, former students of mine and good friends, committed $1,000. There were gifts from neighbors of ours, and from a pastor who one day after a prayer meeting we both attended and met at for the first time wrote a check for $100. There was a gift from a friend who led a campaign to get folks to give their loose change jars toward the vision. It resulted in about $500 given. There was a partner church that took up a special offering that led to another $500 gift. And I could go on and on and on with stories like that. It had always been my sense that the money would come from a large group of people who gave smaller gifts rather than from a few people who would give large gifts. Slowly a community was beginning to stir to make this vision come alive.

As the summer wore on, the expected rise in temperatures that usually hit in July and August never really came. People were constantly commenting on what a cool summer we were having. I counted this as a great blessing considering all the running I had to do. While I am not convinced that God would do something like that for just one person, I knew that I still had to thank Him for this unexpected gift.

The runs were beginning to lengthen out in July. By the end of the month I had hit that point in the training schedule where I faced weeks in a row of back-to-back long runs of three to five hours on Mondays and Tuesdays. The training was beginning to get more and more difficult and rather tedious. Yet one of the wonderful benefits of these long runs was the lengthy quiet time all by myself. There was nothing else to do during these times but to run. I could enjoy nature and birds singing. I ran through rainstorms and some powerful thunderstorms. I didn't answer a cell phone or an e-mail. I simply kept my feet moving for significant portions of the afternoons of many weekdays. But these times also had a challenge to them. There were many days where I was overwhelmed by the unknown territory of accomplishing the fifty miles of running and by how far I had to go in my fundraising.

As I ran numerous times through the neighborhood surrounding our home in River Forest, I would often run across other runners and walkers. There is a common bond between people when they are running or walking and passing one another. Often we would greet each other briefly or share an encouraging word about the run or walk or the day's weather.

There was one couple in particular that I started to encounter on a weekly basis at about five o'clock in the evening around the neighborhood. Sometimes I would run across them while they were running and at other times while they were walking. They were always very friendly in their greeting. Finally, one day I ended up encountering them a couple of times in the same evening. As I passed them for the second time, the man called out to me inquiring about what I was training for. I decided to stop and introduce myself and tell them about my vision. Again, they were encouraging and wanted to contribute if they could, but I didn't have any information in print to give them. I told them to try to remember my name and simply Google it along with the words "fifty-mile run," and my website just might come up. We parted ways, encountered each other one more time that night, and then I never saw them again. After telling my wife about this couple, over the next several weeks of not seeing them I simply forgot about them. But they were to come back into my life in a very unexpected way.

The local newspaper decided to run a story on my run. While the story did not include information on the website where people could give, there was enough information about the vision and how it was connected to World Vision, along with my own name, that someone could find the website if they had to. And this couple did. They showed up one day on the giving site along with a donation and a brief note that said, "nice to have met you on your journey." In my mind, only God could have orchestrated the circumstances that led to that encounter and later connection. A community was being used to encourage me and to grow the vision.

September brought me to just over a month before the fifty-mile day of Sunday, October 11. It was at this point in the preparation that doubt started to storm me with a fierceness that I couldn't turn away. The training schedule was getting difficult and tiresome. The fundraising was stuck at about $7,000 or so. I faced a six-to-seven hour run within the next couple of weeks. I began to wonder if I was some sort of fool for taking this all on. What if I didn't even come close to the $50,000? What if I couldn't really run all fifty miles? After all, I wouldn't attempt that full distance until the actual day of the run.

All along I had continued to send out e-mails and Facebook messages to all of my contacts keeping them up to date on how I was doing on my journey. But everything seemed stuck and stagnant. I had been working on this vision and dream for over five months. The freshness of the excitement and passion had worn off. But, of course, in an unexpected and unplanned fashion, hope stirred again.

Ryan and Sara Hall had loosely stayed in touch with the vision to start the running mentoring club for at-risk kids and adults through Team World Vision National Director, Michael Chitwood. At various times he shared the vision with one or both of them, a vision he and I had talked about for nearly five years. I had also had an opportunity to go for a lakefront run with Ryan and Michael when Ryan was in town doing some sponsorship work around one of Chicago's half marathon events. During this run all three of us chatted about the excitement we had around this vision for the running mentoring club. Some weeks later, Michael called me to tell me that Ryan and Sara wanted to give a significant contribution via their foundation toward getting the running mentoring club started in Chicago.

The storm of doubts began to quiet as God continued to surprise me with His plans in the midst of the weaknesses of my humanness. Near the end of September, the fundraising total began to push past $30,000. Suddenly people remembered the vision. Suddenly people began to see that this dream and vision was on the move and they wanted to be a part of it. There were seven of us total who were raising money particularly for the $50,000 goal. Every one of them but me was simply running the marathon part of the 50-mile run. This goal finally seemed to be reachable because a community of givers and difference-makers was stirring.

By the beginning of October, the fundraising total was approaching $45,000. The money had come in through the total team effort of the seven of us. But I was still hopeful that my own personal goal of $50,000 could be met. Team World Vision held a dinner celebration two nights before the October 11 Sunday morning Chicago Marathon. When that day arrived our team total had come to almost $58,000, and my personal part of that had reached just over $48,000. God had used the smallness of my courage to accept a call to shake the world toward a better place. God had used hundreds to get it done. We are always better as a community than we ever are on our own.

As the day of the fifty-mile run came, I had logged nearly 2,500 miles of running. I had done more than thirty runs of over fifteen miles. My journey was the journey of a community. My journey became the story of God at work in and through everyday, ordinary people. But one big day still loomed over me with all of its challenges.

**Key Insights: Write a few insights here or in your journal/notebook.**

_____

_____

_____

## Run/Walk/Ride to Pray

# BIBLE MEDITATION: EXODUS 4:1–17

**Key Insights: Write a few insights here or in your journal/notebook.**

---

---

---

## Run/Walk/Ride to Listen:

GOD LOVES TO move in unexpected and surprising ways. His movement in this way becomes a joyful gift to people and leads to His story being more prominent than that of any one individual. Yet there is no way around the commitment and discipline it takes to act on a vision even when you believe God is at work over and above what you could ever imagine or get done by yourself. And with every step of discipline and commitment that it takes to move toward accomplishing your visions and dreams to help better our world, there will be doubts, fears, and weariness that climb into your mind and heart as unwanted inhabitants. That is why God often starts by moving in one person, but then uses that one person to stir up a community of relationships. The ultimate joy of a vision is in the team of people that are used together to get it done. We need each other's gifts, encouragement, and energy. We truly do feed off of one another.

So, go for a run, walk, or bike ride today and use the quiet time to offer your authentic fears, doubts, and aloneness to God. Humbly ask Him to send people your way who will surprise you with their gifts and encouragement toward the accomplishment of your vision. Maybe as you pass other people walking or running, greet them with a word of encouragement just as you hope for that to come your way. As you pass them, remember that God will be faithful to you in the dark moments of loneliness and doubt, and just at the right time you will encounter who it is He is sending to you to keep you going on your journey.

**Key Insights: Write a few insights here or in your journal/notebook.**

_____

_____

_____

# BIBLE MEDITATION: EXODUS 15

**Key Insights: Write a few insights here or in your journal/notebook.**

---

---

---

## Risk to Live:

PERSEVERANCE IS ONE of my favorite words. For some reason I have been given the gift of perseverance. It is a deep part of my nature. In the early years of my life, I would most often express that perseverance in sports that I played. I would put out effort in whatever game I was playing that was like a reckless abandonment toward whatever it took to compete or win, or to simply do the very best I could. Perseverance is risky. It usually costs something in terms of time, effort, emotions, and physical output. But that is truly how the world will be shifted for the better—by all kinds of people using their gifts in the midst of one call or several calls to get something done toward some pain or struggle in our world.

Today I challenge you to persevere in your call, dream, and vision. I ask that you once again in a journal or below write down how you will sustain or renew or start an effort toward a stirring that never quite seems to leave you. And along the way, enjoy the surprising discovery of others God sends your way who share a piece of that vision and contribute toward its accomplishment. Don't forget to write down those stories too. Don't forget to write down how your story and journey became that of a community. Don't miss how the journey is ultimately one that is the unexpected story of God at work in His world.

**Write about your need for a support community here or in your journal/notebook.**

---

---

---

## Run/Walk/Ride to Pray

# PART VI

## STEP BY STEP: ACTING ON THE VISION/DREAM

*One step at a time is all that's possible—even when those steps are taken on the run.*

—Anne W. Schaef
writer and lecturer[1]

# BIBLE MEDITATION: GENESIS 12:1–9

**Key Insights: Write a few insights here or in your journal/notebook.**

_____

_____

_____

### Reflect to Hear:

IT IS NOT uncommon for me to get overwhelmed by an idea, vision, or dream because I am looking too far ahead. When I look too far ahead I see a mountain of decisions and things to get done. Then I begin to worry and get anxious. Those feelings steal sleep and energy. And if I entertain them for too long I get frozen and don't even take a step toward my vision or dream. I often get the feeling that many dynamic visions have fallen flat for many people because they are overwhelmed by what they can't control or predict. They look at the end and can't imagine what it will take to organize and accomplish the means to get there. Their passion is then stunted and nothing gets done. And nothing in their life or the world changes. That's why the age-old advice to take one step at a time is so very true and helpful. Yes, you and I need to know where we are going, what the end looks like. But there is often too much time, too many variables, and too little we can control about the in-between from start to finish.

When I take on something of significance that could lead to great results but requires tremendous work, trust, and effort, I often find that after a while I must simply take the first step in order to get moving. It is often the first step that reveals the next one or two. And when I take the first step, my confidence has a chance to grow or adjust. Suddenly I can begin to imagine that this vision can get done by taking one step at a time, by breaking down the vision into smaller pieces. And often I think this is how God grows faith: "I have to let go of the rope." And when my faith grows, I get to know more about God. And when I get to know more about God, I am willing to take more steps of risk and faith. One step at a time remains steady, tried wisdom.

**Key Insights: Write a few insights here or in your journal/notebook.**

_____

_____

_____

Run/Walk/Ride to Pray

# BIBLE MEDITATION: GENESIS 15

**Key Insights: Write a few insights here or in your journal/notebook.**

_____

_____

_____

## Read to Think:

WE GATHERED AT a Starbucks parking lot 23.8 miles out from the start of the Chicago Marathon at 1:30 a.m. for a time of prayer. I was shocked to see that about ten people or so had chosen to gather with the thirteen of us that would be traveling these first miles together. It was only thirty degrees—much colder than I had ever anticipated, even when I thought it could possibly be cold. We were bundled to the point where we could only see each other's faces. My wife, two daughters, and future daughter-in-law were in a car that would be in front of us this entire leg of the run. My sister and her husband and our church's youth pastor road in a vehicle that would follow us. And my son, son-in-law, and another friend were riding bikes alongside me. And one good friend from out of state came down and had pledged to run the entire first 23.8 miles with me. His wife followed at the back end in a vehicle as well. Later another friend would join me at about the eight mile mark and run to the start of the marathon as well. At 1:45 a.m. we entered Roosevelt Road just west of Route 53 in the suburb of Glen Ellyn, Illinois. It was cold, quiet, and calm with little traffic—at least for a few moments.

Just thirty hours earlier our entire family and a few friends had celebrated the fundraising accomplishments of the members of Team World Vision at an evening dinner. The dinner was attended by about five hundred people and served as a sort of rally for the Sunday morning marathon that all of us would be running. It was a great evening of inspiration and also brought awareness to the "run" that I would be doing leading up to the marathon that we would all be doing together.

It was a great evening of celebrating and eating but I was beginning to get very nervous about the mountain of miles that were ahead of me. All of us went home that night sensing that there was a path ahead of us that was unknown territory, no matter what part of it we were involved in. I slept well that Friday night—my last good night's sleep for twenty-four hours.

Saturday was both the same as it always was and yet mysteriously different. I attempted, like everyone else in my family, to go about my usual routine. Saturdays were typically laid back and relaxed for us. My wife would attend a YMCA exercise class while I waited for her to be done and meet me at a local coffee shop. We would then return home for some house cleaning and reading and relaxing. During most of the day we didn't really talk much about what was ahead. Everything was planned and there really was no more to do. We could not control what we didn't know.

While we were home that day I got a call from a news anchor from our local NBC affiliate. She was going to be doing live interviews before the start of the marathon. She had gotten connected to my story in a very unique way. Our son, Aaron, works at a local running gear store. While he was at work on Thursday morning, she walked into the store asking about some warm clothing to prepare her for the thirty-degree temperature of the next day's marathon. Aaron had no idea who she was and asked her if she would be running. She told him no and then shared that she was an early morning news anchor for NBC and would be doing interviews at the start line of the marathon. Aaron's mind immediately went into action. He told her that he had a story for her that she wouldn't want to miss. As he shared with her about the fifty-mile run, she wondered why she hadn't heard about this earlier. She then insisted that she get in touch with me and try to do an interview after the first 23.8 miles and before I started the marathon portion of my fifty-mile run. Aaron then gave her my cell phone number.

She and I chatted for a few moments Saturday morning about the neighborhood we shared and, of course, the run ahead. She very kindly asked if it was at all possible for me to make it to the front start area of the marathon to be her first interview of the morning when she went live at 7 a.m. I told her that I couldn't guarantee anything because there were so many variables, but that Aaron, who would be with me on his bike, would call her the minute we arrived in the start area. She gave me her cell phone number with the hopes that this would all work out. She then pledged to follow the story of the running club after the marathon as well.

As the day continued on, my inner intensity continued to grow. I wondered if it would even be possible to go to sleep at all later that evening. I continued to find small things to do to keep myself occupied and not overwhelmed by the many hours and miles ahead. Our family sat down that evening for one more pre-race meal that would be filled with potential energy for the night and day we would be largely spending on the streets of metro Chicago. At about 8:30 I attempted to settle myself down enough to lie down for some rest and possible sleep. The first hour or so was one of quiet thoughtfulness about all that had led up to the fifty-mile challenge. What a ride it had been. Miles of training, many unexpected encounters with people, hundreds of donors participating, and yet so much still unknown. Finally, at about 9:30, I drifted off to a light sleep only to awaken about two hours later ready to get going.

A little after midnight my son-in-law, John, and my daughter, Leah, arrived from their home. That got us all moving and ready to go with a near giddy spirit of adventure as we faced the darkness of the night. We left our home at 12:45 unsure of whether anyone would come out to join us for our planned prayer time at 1:30 a.m. Our car's thermometer registered thirty degrees. It was calm but it was frosty. But the blessing was that there was no rain in the forecast. As we pulled up to the Starbucks in Glen Ellyn, we were stunned by the many friends who had come out to join us at such an odd hour. My spirits were lifted immediately upon seeing everyone. All of us seemed to have a sense of joyful adventure about us. At 1:30 we gathered everyone, and I shared a few words of thanks for their love and support. We joined hands in a circle and prayed. A few minutes later our caravan of three vehicles, four bikers, and two runners entered the nearly abandoned Roosevelt road. It was cold, quiet, mysterious, serene, and strange.

Suddenly and nearly out of nowhere, five squad cars from the Lombard police appeared to escort us through their community. We were all stunned at this unexpected gift. One car pulled up behind our group, another on the side, one in front and a couple ready to block every intersection. Because our pace was quite deliberate—eleven minutes of running and one minute walking—we were often able to converse with the police who rode next to us. We told them how thankful we were that they would take the time to do this, and they replied that this was the stuff they loved to do.

And as we arrived at the border of Lombard, we could see ahead that the next village's police were ready to offer the same guidance and protection—lights flashing and intersections blocked so that we never really had to hesitate. This same experience happened over and over as we passed from one town to the next. Not only was it entertaining for all of us, but very humbling. It simply wasn't expected. A couple of weeks earlier I had attended a monthly community coalition meeting called the Westside Minister's Coalition and shared my schedule of where I would be and at what time with friends in the Oak Park police and Chicago police. The Oak Park officer informed me that he would let all of the suburban departments know what I was up to. And a week earlier a deputy chief of the Chicago department let me know that they would keep an eye on me through Chicago. But I never expected that they would offer the protection they did for just an ordinary guy like myself. I was blessed by their plan and the sense that God was definitely overseeing this day.

I started the run a bit faster than I had planned. That was partly due to wanting to keep moving in the cold and partly due to the flow of my adrenaline. At first it was difficult to build in the minute walk per every mile. It turned into more of a minute every two to three miles. Deep in my mind I knew this wasn't a good idea but I still struggled with this discipline. And as the run continued I started getting warmer and warmer, and eventually stopped to remove my long running pants. It was then that our group of runners and bikers settled into a better and steady pattern—eleven minutes of running, one minute of walking. This resulted in a pace of a little over five miles an hour. My hope was to arrive at the Team World Vision Charity tent at about 6:30 to 6:40. I would then have about forty-five minutes to eat and get to my start area for the Chicago marathon. At this early point I wasn't sure if that would include enough time to do the NBC interview with the news anchor I had spoken with Saturday morning.

The miles clicked off quickly and steadily. Every mile or so my son or son-in-law would ride their bike back to me and check on how I was doing and whether or not I needed anything. I was trying to eat some gel blocks and/or a nutrition bar every couple of miles. I had also been planning on drinking water or Gatorade steadily, but found that

I wasn't nearly as conscious of my thirst or need for liquid because it was so cold.

Along the way I was blessed to have regular conversations with my running partner, Steve. Steve and his wife had driven down from Michigan to be a part of this event. They and their children had been longtime family friends and former members of our church community. Weeks earlier Steve had asked me if it would be helpful to have him run the first 23.4 miles with me. I welcomed the company. Others had talked about jumping in to run some of the miles, but no one had made a definite commitment other than Steve. The greatest challenge for Steve during these miles was the slow pace that I was doing for the run. Running slower is often more difficult for runners because it is a bit unnatural when you still feel very fresh or if you had trained at a much quicker pace. The time with Steve was both an encouragement and a treasure that I will hold deep in my heart for years to come.

Besides having my son and son-in-law ride alongside me and having other family members and friends in the vehicles, one of the great unexpected joys was having two other bike riders join us as well—Tony and Phil. I enjoyed the times they would pull up next to me at various times during the run and chat about all kinds of topics.

The joy and entertainment of the change of police protection continued to keep the run moving along quickly but we also enjoyed the occasional shout from a passing vehicle. The shouts or horn beeps were always done in an encouraging fashion because of the police presence. We were also quite entertained by one rather inebriated pedestrian walking a slow, crooked path on the side of the road going the opposite direction of us. I wondered if the police would pause to have a chat with him, but they let him be in order to stay with us. As we crossed under the 294 tollway, we came across a bar very close to the road. Many of the patrons were outside for a smoke or came out when they saw all the flashing police lights. One patron even yelled to us, "What are you guys doing?" We shouted back, as if it were a normal Sunday at 3 a.m. activity, "We're running and riding bikes." We received an ongoing perplexed stare but no reply.

At about the ten mile mark we approached a cemetery alongside the road, where we were met by another friend who had contacted me to see if he could run some of the miles with me. Jeff was the husband of a former supervisor I had when I was the chaplain at a local Christian college. I had gotten to know Jeff over the years and we both enjoyed exchanging runner's stories. Jeff had run over a dozen plus marathons scattered across the country. He became a welcome third runner in our group and brought a new sense of energy and encouragement to us with fifteen miles to go before the start area of the marathon. His wife, Ginny, who had come to drop Jeff off, in her usual enthusiastic fashion, shouted encouragement as we passed her.

With about ten miles to go, we ran past an intersection that was no more than two or three miles from our home. It was a small, reflective moment that marked how far I had come from five months ago when I made a public commitment to this vision. It was strange to run past familiar businesses and homes knowing that I would not return to the area for another twelve hours or so. I still had seven or eight more hours of running ahead of me. At this point it also became an ongoing joke for all of us running and biking that we passed closed restaurants that served food that always seemed to sound good to us even though it was the early morning hours of a Sunday that was still filled with darkness. We really did want the pizza and the hot dogs. And we wanted to eat every loaf of bread we could get our hands on as we passed a local bread company in the midst of baking. The smells nearly pulled us off the road with a desire to dive into the bags of bread we imagined being prepared.

At this point in the run it was very striking to notice how empty the streets were. We were getting closer and closer to the city of Chicago, which meant that on a normal day Roosevelt Road would have been filled with cars and people seeking to catch buses or walk to local stores. It was about 4:15 a.m. and it was generally quiet and barren on this normally bustling street. The only noise was that of the support vehicles, bikes, the pounding of our running shoes on the pavement, and the ongoing movement of the police vehicles all around us. The rhythm of these sounds continued for the next couple of miles until we crossed the border into another village, watching the police of the previous village peel back to care for more important things within their borders of responsibility. And then something happened that had not taken place during the entire trip up to this point. There were no police that had joined us for this part of the journey. They had been so unexpectedly faithful up to this point that this took us by complete surprise. In fact, we were a bit scared for the first time. We simply felt more vulnerable in the quiet and empty street. Suddenly it seemed that we were responsible for our safety and plan.

We were now only a mile or so from the border of the city of Chicago. None of us had any idea of what to expect when we crossed into Chicago. While I had informed the police that I would be running through the city on this section of Roosevelt Road, my understanding was that at the most there might be an officer or two that would keep an eye on us periodically. And suddenly seemingly out of nowhere a lone squad car appeared to escort us through the final eight hundred meters before we hit Cicero Avenue, the official border of Chicago. And as we ran each meter we could increasingly see what appeared to be a large number of blue flashing lights. My first thought was that something had happened near the upcoming intersection and we would have to enter through the area rather cautiously. But as we got closer it became obvious that nothing at all had happened—they were waiting for us.

As we came to the city limits gateway of Chicago, six Chicago police cars were awaiting our arrival. This was beyond anything I could have imagined. The traditional flashing blue lights of the Chicago police were nearly blinding. We could hardly believe what we were seeing. Throughout the run I had always been thinking that they must have had more important things to do than this. Didn't they realize that I was just an ordinary, everyday guy who had planned this event entirely on his own? But as we greeted every village's police officers who had come to escort us, the statement was always the same: "We love doing this kind of stuff and we hope you do very well." And the Chicago police were no different. As we greeted them, they too indicated that they were glad to help. I would certainly have to thank the Chicago police officer who had helped set up all the Chicago guidance down Roosevelt Road, much to my surprise, along with the Oak Park officer who had set up the guidance during the suburban stretch. When we had first talked about it I got the sense that there would be a couple of officers who would keep an eye on us throughout the run through Chicago. But I could have not imagined what actually happened.

The journey through Chicago was an amazing one. The Chicago police not only blocked each intersection that we ran through, but they blocked the entire road behind us and in front of us. No one, not even a city bus, was allowed around us. Traffic backed up behind us as we traveled through the city. One of the other incredible surprises was being met by some good friends, Bethany and Cyndee, who had trekked to this area to cheer us on at several intersections. We were also joined by my good friend, Cini, on her bike. She stayed with us until we arrived near the starting area of the marathon. These friends would cheer at one intersection, hop in their car and get ahead of us, waiting until we arrived at another intersection. They repeated this several times. I was so encouraged by this joyous and surprising gift. One of the other persons cheering was Deb, who was from Austin Corinthian Baptist Church. She and her husband and family had become our dear friends over the years of our churches' partnership. It was such a great blessing to see her there that morning as we passed near their church location.

As we got closer and closer to the center of the city, traffic was increasing, and we were very glad that the police were escorting us through what were becoming rather dangerous street conditions. Another great gift was given by a former World Vision colleague and friend, who lives in the South Loop area of the city and met us on his bike. He was taking several pictures and some video footage of the run. One of the pieces of video that he caught was at one intersection where a driver attempted to break through the police vehicles as they blocked the intersection for us to pass through. I am not sure what happened to that driver, but the police were not at all happy with his move. As the police got out of their cars yelling at him, we moved on quickly through this intersection. My former World Vision colleague captured most of this on video and later posted it on YouTube. This fifteen-second video that we watched later gave us a great laugh and memory from the run.

Eventually, we arrived only a couple of blocks from the start area and charity village area of the marathon. The vehicles carrying my wife, family, and friends had to break off and park so they could get on the course to continue cheering once the marathon started. The two runners, Steve and Jeff, also gave me their goodbyes. They had done such a gracious job of staying with me and keeping me going during these early miles. My son and son-in-law continued on with me on their bikes. And just as we got to within a block or so of the charity village area, my destination, we were joined by blaring sirens of motor-cycle police escorting me right to the entrance to the village.

The three of us entered the charity village area after 23.8 miles of cold, dark running and biking. We suddenly saw the World Vision tent in sight. A call had been made ahead of us that we were close to arriving. As I came to the tent people started cheering both out-side of the tent and inside, welcoming us to the anticipation of the marathon to come. After several congratulations and hugs, I quickly found the two runners, Annette and Maddie, who would be joining me for the marathon portion of the run. I greeted them quickly and found my gear bag so I could get a quick break and grab some nutrition. I really couldn't settle in too much. There were still 26.2 miles to run and I also needed to get to an interview with NBC 5 near the very front of the start area of the marathon. The journey to the front of the marathon start area was one of great chaos. Thousands of people were milling around the start area waiting for the marathon to begin. We also needed to keep calling the NBC anchor and interviewer for clearance through several checkpoints.

This trek took us nearly the entire hour that I had before the start of the marathon. Upon arriving at the professional runner start area, the NBC news anchor welcomed me with a big hug and greeting. She said we had just a few minutes before I would be her first interview of the morning coverage of the marathon. The cue came and I did a brief two or three minute interview about why I was doing the fifty-mile run and how it had gone up to this point. Then quickly we left again to get back to the start area we were given for the marathon. Little did I realize that due to the cold and change from running to walking and stopping, my leg muscles locked up as tight as a drum.

We arrived back at the "ordinary" person start area and prepared to be off with the sound of the start horn in just a few minutes. The horn blew and then...we waited. It always takes about five minutes before you move forward with some thirty thousand-plus people moving in the same direction. Slowly we inched forward, walking step by step. Eventually the pace picked up to a faster walk, then a light jog, and finally to a near easy running pace. It took us about twelve minutes to reach the official start line. It was only then that we could have enough space to begin running with any kind of speed.

But as soon as we started I knew that these next many miles would be a great challenge. My leg muscles had stiffened up and gotten sore in the thirty degree cold. Annette and Maddie, who were running with me, immediately had to slow up their pace to wait for me. Not only were my leg muscles cold and stiff, but there was a lot of pain with each running step forward. It appeared that these next twenty-six miles would be very tedious and difficult. I remained hopeful that everything would loosen up in the first few miles, but in the first mile already it became clear that this likely would not happen.

I struggled my way through these opening steps of the marathon portion of my run. I had now begun to enter mile twenty-four of the fifty miles. The first nearly twenty-four miles had gone so well and so smoothly that it was understandable that these miles would be much more difficult. We once again met up with my family and friends at the three mile mark. They were excited to see me and Annette and Maddie after now having been separated for about an hour plus since they broke off from the first half of the run. At this point they couldn't really tell that I was struggling. Or if they did they likely just thought that it was still early enough in the marathon that things could change. I took the time to greet everyone—now a crowd that not only included my family but also many friends that had met up with them. We chatted briefly. I got some more nutrition via a banana, energy bar, and some Gatorade. We then had to keep moving since we had at least another four and half hours of running to do.

As we moved forward into the fourth mile, I started looking forward to my plan of running ten minutes and walking for two. Nothing was loosening up at all. I then began to worry about Annette and Maddie and whether they would have the patience to deal with me over these next twenty-two miles or so. But they remained devoted and indicated that this was the commitment they made—to run with me for encouragement during the marathon portion, no matter what.

While I struggled on and off during this first half of the marathon, the joy of it was the size of the crowds and the encouragement of fellow runners. For the first half of any marathon, all the runners are feeling great. The crowd is enthusiastic since they have not yet been waiting for hours for a particular runner they have been looking for. The various ethnic and cultural neighborhoods that you run through are also always a treat. During the twenty-six-mile Chicago course you end up running through about eighteen different ethnic neighborhoods or distinct communities that have their own very unique flavor.

Another surprising encouragement that came my way was the number of spectators and runners that encouraged me along the way. Many of them had either heard about my fifty-mile run or had even seen the interview that I did that morning. They would often shout out to me with enthusiasm as I passed. And I was enjoying all of this as much as I could, but I was really struggling with tiredness, stiffness, and pain. All of these began to take their toll on me, and for the first time in the midst of my running, I began to wonder if I could actually get through all fifty miles.

As we pushed our way to the ten mile mark, I was continuing to struggle and often lengthen out my walk times. But I also looked forward to getting back into the Loop area of the city where I would again see my family and friends. This hope sustained me as we plodded along through these miles. Each aid station became a gift to me every couple of miles because not only did it mean some nutrition through Gatorade, but it also meant I could walk again in order to be able to drink.

As we neared the downtown loop area of the city, I suddenly remembered that World Vision had teamed up with Moody radio to set up a cheer station at the eleven mile mark. Once again I had something to look forward to that came even before I would see my family. But I received an earlier boost from a surprise cheerer. My friend, Rick, suddenly came out onto the course at about the ten mile mark and not only greeted us, but, with a backpack loaded on his back, he ran with us for the next many miles. And then, to my even greater surprise, when I arrived at the World Vision cheer station I spotted my mom and dad along with LuAnn, a dear friend who had taken them to the city so they could be a part of witnessing the fifty miles and encouraging me along the way. I quickly ran over to them and hugged each one of them. This was a great distraction that kept me from thinking about the pain I was in. I was also so blessed to know that my parents were really behind me as I took on this great adventure.

Finally, we arrived at the 12 to 12.5 mile mark where I knew my family and friends would be camped out. They had endured waiting nearly three hours for me to arrive at this point of my run—which was the thirty-five mile mark of the total run. I could tell that it had been a long, cold wait in the nearly thirty-degree weather. The sun had never come out as predicted and there was a subtle wind always throwing itself around us. But they were very excited and enthusiastic as we arrived and ran over to the side to greet them. And quickly they could see that I was struggling. At this point I was not happy and I was ready to cry. All the emotion and perseverance was beginning to roll over me. Later I learned that Annette had pulled some of them aside and told them truthfully how much I was hurting. But they all tried to stay positive. I also learned later that Laura and others began to text friends and family to be praying for me since it appeared that I was in severe trouble toward meeting the fifty mile goal.

Once again I tried to eat as much as I could with the hope that the food would stir my energy and muscles to somehow make a shift toward new life. I remember at one point, in near tears, saying out loud that you really can't know the Resurrection (of Christ) if you don't know suffering. And I really did believe that in part I was suffering by the allowance of God. This suffering would continue to teach me about dependence on Him rather than myself. I was living out the principle that He would have to come on me in power in the midst of my emotional, spiritual, and physical weakness if I was to ever complete this vision. It wasn't until days after the marathon was over that I would see myself saying these words via a video recording that a friend had taken on his iPhone. When I saw that part of the video I too could see how much I was suffering at that time. Finally, after about ten to fifteen minutes of resting I departed again with Annette and Maddie to journey on to reach the goal of fifty miles. I had "only" fifteen to go.

We were quickly greeted and cheered by the crowd that is always so large and strong in the Loop area of the course. And then as we passed the 13.1 mile mark, the official halfway point of the marathon, I suddenly mysteriously sensed that something was changing. I slowly discovered that I had new energy, new joy, and new vision. I had no idea how it came upon me—God mysteriously at work not only applying the nutrition of the food I had eaten, but going much, much further inside me. But I didn't really care where it had come from. I just knew that something had changed and it felt so very good. I began to run with new legs. I got back to a smoother routine of running ten minutes and walking two minutes. The next five miles seemed to move along with a whole sense of newness to them. I had somehow broken through "the wall."

Again, we arrived at the next place of meeting for family and friends—the seventeen mile mark of the marathon. The group could not believe their eyes or their watches. I had just done that five miles in one hour. They could literally see the change that had come over me. I was smiling. I was joking. And...and...the sun had come out! Everyone responded to my new spirit with great joy and laughter. And I wanted some M&Ms! It was as if that treat met up with my new and fresh emotions. My son, Aaron, then grabbed me and said, "Dad, do you realize that you have now run further than you ever have? You are at the forty mile mark!" Those words spilled over me with deep amazement. And it was at that point for the first time on the marathon portion of the fifty-mile run that I knew that I was going to make it to the end. I suddenly knew that I could run, walk, crawl, or drag my body to the end. I knew then that God was showing me the end of the journey before I even got there.

It was also at this point in the marathon that I received my next great surprise. My wife pointed out to me that Larry and Ruth, Laura's brother and his wife, were with them. I quickly and joyfully greeted them with my newfound energy. They had big smiles on their faces. I remember telling them about the best t-shirt I ever saw on a marathon runner. It said, "If I had married a Kenyan, I would be eating lunch right now." Most Kenyan runners completed the marathon in under two hours and fifteen minutes. I also had one concern at this point, however. Annette had fallen back to find a Porta-John® and had not yet caught up to Maddie and myself. I was afraid we had lost her somehow. But of even more concern was the pain that had developed in her knee. Suddenly, I discovered that I was now more concerned about her than I was about myself. Maddie and I were not sure what to do, but finally decided we needed to run on. And so, after a much shorter break than the earlier one, Maddie and I, along with Rick, departed to finish up the last ten miles of both the marathon and the fifty-mile run.

The next few miles, with Rick at my side and Maddie keeping an eye open for Annette, seemed to move along quite quickly. My energy remained high and I seemed to be able to either do a very fast speed walk that was more like a slow jog, or simply do my run/walk rhythm. And then, to our great surprise, we bumped into Annette. She had somehow passed us, not seeing that we had pulled over to the side where our family and friends were. She had been looking for us, and by God's grace had just turned back and spotted us. It was also at this point that we ran across some friends that had much earlier that morning cheered me in the darkness of the first twenty-four miles. Bethany and Cyndee were volunteers at one of the next aid stations. It was so great to see them again. I was filled with deep humility at their greeting and at their devotion to help all through my run.

More quickly than I had expected, we were approaching the twenty mile mark. Many of my fellow runners joined me in the struggle of this late part of the run. I was always taken aback by some runners who said out loud, "Hey, that's the fifty-mile guy and he's passing us.

We can't let that happen." It is right about at this point in the marathon that you are typically hitting the infamous "wall." It is also at the twenty mile mark that you begin to enter the very entertaining Chinatown neighborhood of Chicago. The Chinatown mile is usually packed with spectators and filled with very loud enthusiasm—along with the great symbolic dragon dancing in the streets. Unexpectedly, my two daughters and son-in-law, who was on his bike, met me in Chinatown to join in the last 6.2 miles. This served to urge me on through this last, increasingly difficult stretch. So, they accompanied me. And Rick, who had helped me through so much, finally departed with his backpack to head back home. He had run/walk/shuffled nearly ten miles with me.

It is at this point in the marathon that runners feel very much alone in their pain as they attempt to break through the wall of exhaustion. This last stretch includes a grueling mile headed south toward U.S. Cellular Field, where the Chicago White Sox play their baseball. Once you arrive near the ballpark you cross over the Dan Ryan Expressway going east, head a bit south again, and then finally east to Michigan Avenue, where you head straight north for the last 2.5 miles.

I was very, very tired for these last three miles. But I was driven by the finish line vision that was etched in my mind. I was also very thankful to have some great companions to help me finish them up. As we turned to head north for the final stretch of miles on Michigan Avenue, I received one more surprise. Jeff, who had run the first 23.8 miles with me, had also volunteered at the last aid station on the course. We briefly greeted each other with great satisfaction that he had been with me for much of the beginning and now saw that I was struggling to the end.

The last couple of miles of a marathon always seem more like five to me. It was a welcome sight to finally see the twenty-five mile mark. The exhausting battle was nearly finished. Somewhere along the way my daughters and son-in-law broke off the course to get over to the finish area. It was Annette, Maddie, and myself left for the last half mile. As we approached the final six hundred meters, there was one barrier left—the Roosevelt Street bridge. I had already run over this bridge at 6:15 that morning as I finished up the first 23.8 miles. It was surreal to be right back there again at nearly two o'clock in the afternoon. Now, this bridge does form a hill. It isn't a really steep hill but it does hurt to run up it at this part of the marathon course—let alone after having run nearly fifty miles. I call it the "hill of swearing." I don't swear much but that hill always makes me bring out every word I have the energy to think of at that point.

I made it to the top of the hill, ran the short down hill, and turned to my left for the final few hundred meters. The big "FINISH" banner was straight ahead. And then suddenly on my right I could hear the cheers of my family and friends. Some of them had endured staying with me from midnight on. Others had made it through thirty-degree temperatures and six hours to meet me at this point—fifty miles. I hugged the right edge of the course and could hear someone yelling "Fifty miles, yeaaaaah!" I slapped each of their hands that greeted me and ran on to cross the finish line with Annette and Maddie close by. It was done! Fifty years old, fifty miles, $50,000.

We slowly made our way through the finish chute area. Our timing chips were removed and we grabbed some food to try to urge on our recovery. I was satisfyingly tired. Gradually, we walked into the Charity Village area, where World Vision had a celebration tent for team runners, family, and friends. As I walked up to the tent, my family was there to greet me. Never had the hugs from each one of them felt so deeply rich and joyful. It had been as much their journey as mine. I was overwhelmed that they had stuck with me through this crazy vision. I was filled with a deep, mysterious love for them.

The next great hug I got was from Michael Chitwood, the Team World Vision National Director and dear, personal friend. He had been a great support along the way. He knew what went into this run. It was not only about me, but about a cause that always sits deep on his and my heart—too many people are struggling for the basics while I relish in the luxuries. It was then that I heard clapping and cheering in the tent—"Tim, Tim, Tim, Tim." As I walked in, I was amazingly greeted by my fellow runners and teammates and their families and friends. I could barely speak. I could hardly handle the attention but yet was thankful. I knew that this run had been so much about God's power in my weakness. I took it that their cheers were more for Him than for me. Thanks be to God!

The time of celebration in the tent was very rich. While I was exhausted, God gave me the strength to talk with many folks who had been touched by what I had done. I was humbled by all of their comments. So many stated that they were inspired to do their marathon because of what I was doing. I was also so grateful to greet a few other runners and friends who had helped raise several thousand dollars to help toward the $50,000. Anthony, Kim, and Craig were a great blessing to me—and to the people of Kenya.

After all of us ate some food and talked with friends, we finally were ready to head home to get ready to collapse. The only challenge was that I still was due to check in at a multi-church gathering that we are a part of on the second Sunday of each month. It was the last thing that I felt I had the energy for but I knew that I must get there. These churches had supported and prayed for me throughout my training and they had helped raise money toward the cause. We got home about 4:30 in the afternoon. We had been up since midnight—nearly seventeen hours. The church gathering wasn't far from our home and started at 5 p.m. I showered and both my wife and I slowly made our way to the car to head to the gathering.

When we walked in the door of Austin Corinthian Baptist church, we were greeted with an overwhelming standing ovation from the people. They represented some six churches that gather regularly across various ethnic, location, and denominational lines. I quickly asked if I could speak right at the beginning of the gathering since I didn't have much energy left. They agreed to allow me to speak right away. I was humbled to share with them all the experiences and lessons of the day and of the entire journey toward the fifty mile day. Mostly I wanted them to know two things: this vision was about God and His power in the midst of my weakness, and that I could never have done it without such faithful friends that had been given to me over so many years—the friends of these churches were black, white, Latino, older, and younger.

One of the most moving responses to the run and the money that was raised for Africa came from a young Liberian girl who had been adopted into the family of one of the pastors that participated in our fellowship of churches. She came up to me that evening at the church gathering and thanked me for giving to Africa, a place so close to her heart. She then handed me a handwritten note from her to me. Later that night I sat down and read this moving letter thanking me for loving the place she came from (read the note in the Appendix). I was humbled because I was actually more stirred by her story of survival than my own survival of the fifty-mile-run vision. And so, I received yet another unexpected and undeserved gift from God through one of His precious people.

Laura and I left after about a forty-five-minute celebration of the day. We returned home to promptly crash in our beds for the rest of the evening and night. I awakened on Monday to discover that I could hardly walk. We live on the third floor of a condo building without an elevator. I had five flights of stairs to either go down or up. I knew however, that it was essential that I walk to get the blood moving through my body in order to encourage healing. So, I gingerly and slowly made my way down the five flights of stairs to go out walking. By the next day I was already 70 percent better, and by the third day of recovery I could have run if I had to. I was amazed by how the body was made not only to endure things like fifty-mile runs, but also to recover from the damage done from them. Once again, I found myself giving credit to God for His power and imaginative creativity! He had inspired the vision of a fifty-mile run. I had just enough willingness to do it. He took that small willingness and did so much more than I could ever ask, do, or imagine. Thanks be to God!

**Key Insights: Write a few insights here or in your journal/notebook.**

_____

_____

_____

Run/Walk/Ride to Pray

# BIBLE MEDITATION: GENESIS 17

**Key Insights: Write a few insights here or in your journal/notebook.**

_____

_____

_____

## Run/Walk/Ride to Listen:

I AM NOT SURE I would have been able to take on the fifty-mile run if the idea hadn't come at me slowly—one step at a time. It took several weeks for the whole idea to come together. It took a couple of months for my wife and other family members to get on board with the idea and vision. Often, in order to become willing to act on a "bigger than me" idea, we can't spend time anticipating all that will take place as we act on the plan. There are so many things that we cannot possibly anticipate. There also may be pain or suffering or things to endure that could quite easily keep us from ever taking one step toward the accomplishment of the vision. This world has always been changing through the rather ignorant efforts of young, idealistic risk takers. Had they always known what was ahead they would have possibly not even taken any action at all. But the other side of it is that even if the vision involves pain and sacrifice, that too is not constant. It usually comes in parts or steps within the overall plan of action.

So today as you run or walk or take a bike ride, envision just taking one step at a time toward the dream or vision you have had seeking to do something big with your one life. Think of it much like your walking, running or riding—one step, one movement of the pedal, one block, one mile, and so forth. Remember that the enacting of your vision is much like this run, walk, or ride—it is a journey that has many twists and turns to it mentally, physically, and emotionally. And it has all of those with much variety in the peaks and valleys.

**Key Insights: Write a few insights here or in your journal/notebook.**

---

---

---

# BIBLE MEDITATION: GENESIS 22

**Key Insights: Write a few insights here or in your journal/notebook.**

_____

_____

_____

## Risk to Live:

ALL IDEAS THAT are so much bigger than ourselves involve pain, or at the very least some difficult barriers one way or another. That is the sacrifice. That is the risk. But the mysterious thing is that God has made human beings with an incredible ability to endure. I am always quite shocked by the stories I read of how much people have endured and lived to talk about. I am amazed by how much we can recover from. As I write this it has been nearly three years since I ran the fifty-mile run and watched over $50,000 come pouring in. The run was difficult; not nearly as difficult as most things that people go through, but it was difficult. It was plain old painful. I had doubts that I could make it. Others doubted I could make it in the midst of its execution. But here I am writing about it. I made it. I endured. I recovered. I am again able to consider new challenges, visions, and dreams that may also involve suffering and overwhelming difficulty. That's the beauty of the one step at a time approach. The old saying that God doesn't give us more than we can handle is generally true. I call out to you today to not allow the potential pain and barriers of your wonders and visions to overwhelm you to the point of hindering you from acting or defeating you in the midst of executing the plan. Stay hopeful. Start. And remember, one step at a time is all that is possible—even when you are running with fervent passion.

**Write about the next persevering step you will take here or in your journal/notebook.**

_____

_____

_____

**Run/Walk/Ride to Pray**

# PART VII

## YOUR STEP OF FAITH: MILES TO RUN BEFORE WE SLEEP

*For when I am weak, then I am strong.*

—2 CORINTHIANS 12:10

*And what does the LORD require of you? To act justly and to love mercy and to walk humbly with your God.*

—MICAH 6:8

# BIBLE MEDITATION: 2 CORINTHIANS 12:1–10

**Key Insights: Write a few insights here or in your journal/notebook.**

_____

_____

_____

IT HAS NOW been over two years since that nearly 2 a.m. start to the fifty-mile run. And here is the wild thing God did through this weak effort and journey: God empowered us to raise more than $58,000 for clean water projects in Africa and to start a running/walking club for kids and adults in a nearby underserved neighborhood. I have been asked many times if I will ever do it again. I am also often referred to now as an "ultra-marathoner." To the first I often say that I don't desire to do something like that again, but if it makes sense from a "God-called" standpoint I would not hesitate. I am not an ultra-marathoner. It is not my plan to start attempting various runs over the 26.2 miles of the marathon. And on many days I wonder if I will stop doing marathons all together and simply return to running for exercise and pleasure three to four times a week.

For now I am committed to running races to raise money for important difference-making efforts. And I still want to exercise regularly to attempt to stay healthy for many years to come. I am also committed to helping others enjoy the gift of exercise and all the joys that come along with it. But most importantly I am steadfastly committed to learning and growing in my journey with and for God in the midst of a community of folks seeking to do the same. It is this journey that I most want to share with others regardless of where they are when it comes to faith. I am a person seeking to live in the humility of open-handedness so that God might mysteriously move through my life to act toward justice, to offer mercy, and to live in humble surrender to God and fellow human beings no matter who they are, what they believe, or what they have done.

Since the fifty-mile run I have continued to learn about that kind of life through a variety of means and people. One of the great surprises of the run was an invitation from Ryan Hall, an Olympic and world-class marathoner, and his wife Sara, also a top American distance runner. I had the privilege of meeting them a couple of times through my connection to World Vision. And initially, after hearing about my efforts through the fifty-mile run, they made a commitment to give a significant donation to my desire to start a running/walking club for kids and adults in a nearby underserved neighborhood in Chicago. But much to my surprise, they started a conversation about possibly having me pilot the program on behalf of a difference-making foundation, called Steps, that they had started. The idea would be that I would be hired to work part-time for the foundation and pilot the program in a neighborhood in Chicago, then spread the program to other neighborhoods in Chicago, and then on to other cities across the US.

This development took me by surprise to say the least. My first reaction was one of being overwhelmed by the prospect. After all, I had two jobs already. But then, at nearly the same time, I learned that the funding for one of my jobs was changing and that I would likely be paid half of what I had been paid in that position. And as Ryan and Sara and I conversed further, it appeared that they would want me to work with them for that exact amount of money. The mystery of living with surrendered open hands before God and man continued beyond anything I could have imagined or asked for!

In March of 2010, I began a quarter-time position with the Hall Steps Foundation. For several months I served as the coordinator of the development of the running, walking, mentoring club here in Chicago. On April 24, 2010 our club was launched in Columbus Park on the west side of Chicago known as the Austin neighborhood. While I no longer work for the Steps foundation, there is a steady group of adults and youth who participate in Saturday morning runs/walks. And many random folks join us on Saturday mornings as we make our way through the park on these runs and walks.

One other thing was stirred up through God empowering my vision. Several Team World Vision runners are now running ultra-marathons to get hundreds of children in Africa sponsored so that they receive the basic necessities of life and experience the power of hope. One group of four runners even ran a total of one hundred miles each in conjunction with the 2011 Chicago Marathon in order to call out for hundreds of children to be sponsored in Kenya. These great efforts are all being done by ordinary people empowered by God to do things beyond themselves to change this world. If I have had any influence on any of this, it is beyond me, and comes to me more as a gift than an achievement.

So here is the bottom line of what I hope you have heard and are wrestling with through my story. I believe that the most important lifestyle decision for the devoted follower of Jesus Christ is to choose to live in the weakness of listening, following, and surrendering to God through the giving up of self-driven and controlled power, influence, and actions. This does not mean leaving behind good, clear thinking and learning. But it does mean to take what is being learned, heard, and thought out, and offering it with humble open hands to the God of the universe, and then waiting on Him to act on that surrender in ways that will mysteriously influence and transform people, structures, and systems to become what they were created to be. This kind of "weakness lifestyle" will lead to lives of acting justly and mercifully with great humility toward God and fellow human beings. And not only will this lifestyle lead to transformation of lives and culture, but it will be an authentic way of living that will give us joy and display the person and work of Jesus to a world that yearns to see Christians walk the talk of that Jesus and His church.

The story above is one that is primarily about my learning to give up to that way of living. And I am still learning with much change to continue to make. I continue to make mistakes in many of my words and actions, which shows how much of a battle this truly is. And this is a lifestyle that is not necessarily encouraged in Western culture, nor in much of the church of Jesus Christ as it is expressed in North America.

These past few years have been filled with exhilarating learning and painful losses, both of which contribute to learning this "weakness lifestyle." I primarily learn from seeking to submit to people who are very different than myself—African-American and Latino leaders here in Chicago, along with many others of various ethnicities and socioeconomic positions—that have not had the privilege that comes along with being a white male in this culture. I also learn from my own church community, which is one of the great treasures and privileges in my life. I also learn every day from my wife and dear children and their spouses. My greatest wish is that I could consistently live in humble listening and receptivity to others that I encounter each day—and that means "all" others.

My main goal of writing down my story of these past few years is to invite you into your own study and investigation of this way of life. I truly believe it will become most satisfying to you, even if filled with difficultly and pain. And so, I offer you this story so that you can begin to record your own as you uniquely join me in this pursuit. I sometimes imagine how the world might change if the church of Jesus Christ sought this way of life. I believe it would have a similar effect as that of Jesus Christ in His own day those two thousand years ago. May God bless you and empower you on the way! And remember, we all have *Miles to "Run" Before We Sleep!*

**Write about your desire to live a life of justice, mercy, humility, and weakness here or in your journal/notebook.**

_____

_____

_____

Run/Walk/Ride to Pray

# FINAL STEPS: TAKING THE RISK TO LIVE AS A CRASH OF RHINOS

*To live without risk is to risk not living.*

— Anonymous

## BIBLE MEDITATION: JOHN 10:7–10

**Key Insights: Write a few insights here or in your journal/notebook.**

_____

_____

_____

THE ABOVE QUOTE came into my life some years ago. It has now become standard living for myself, my wife, my family, and my church—in various ways that are unique to each individual, and husband/wife/family. The way I often think about risk these days is through the example of the rhino.

It is my understanding that the rhino is a very powerful animal that can run around thirty miles an hour. That is about the speed of a squirrel. But the rhino has another interesting trait—it can only see about thirty feet ahead of itself. So now, think about a charging rhino that is always trusting that the thirty-first foot will be OK when it arrives there on its charge. More than likely that is how a group of rhinos became known as a "crash." That, I think, is a great picture of what it takes to live with risk. Risk always involves unknowns, adventure, faith, and trust to one degree or another. And risk also can involve pain, mistakes, and difficulty. But it also has great reward as you follow its journey! There truly is no living without taking risks, in my opinion.

We seem to be entering a time in history that will be filled with change. And I want to invite you to keep the mental picture of the charging rhino as you not only live into those changes, but also as you write down your stirrings, story, and vision in the space that follows or in your journal/notebook. Use the exercises and insights you worked with earlier as a guide to write your entire story down. Listen, pray, watch, follow, learn, be humble, and act with risk and faith. The world needs you!

**Run/Walk/Ride to Pray**

# YOUR STIRRINGS, YOUR STORY, YOUR VISION

*Writing It Down in Detail*

THIS IS THE place to take all the reflecting and writing that you have done throughout the devotional weeks and out on the runs, walks, or bike rides. It is time to put it all down on paper in more detail. You may also choose to write your story in your own journal/ notebook. A friend of mine says that it doesn't exist if it isn't written down. It needs to be written to be seen, to be read, to be acted upon. It then can be a public record where you can live and tell God's great story alive through your life.

# Appendix

# LINDA'S LETTER TO ME

**Dear Tim,**

I hope you will receive the few words I have to say from my heart. Of course, it's not much in comparison to the cash other people will be giving. I hope you will accept it with the same warm heart. I am so happy for you that God gave you the strength to accomplish what you wanted to do. You don't know how that blesses my heart for me to know that somebody would sacrifice their energy. To know that your body may hurt for months just to run for my people in Kenya. It is good to know they have good water to drink day and night. You don't know how much that means to me. I don't know how to say thank you enough. Thank you so much. May God bless you and your family. I hope and pray with all my heart that God will give you the courage and strength to continue the wonderful job you and your family are doing.

**Blessings,**

**Linda**

# NOTES

### Introduction

1. Marva J. Dawn, Powers, *Weakness, and the Tabernacling of God* (Grand Rapids: Wm. B. Eerdmans Publishing Co., 2001).

### Part I, Week #2

1. Shane Claiborne, *The Irresistible Revolution* (Grand Rapids: Zondervan, 2006).

### Part II

1. Brennan Manning, *The Signature of Jesus* (Colorado Springs, CO: Multnomah, 1988).

### Part III

1. Dietrich Bonhoeffer, *The Cost of Discipleship* (New York: Touchstone, 1995).

### Part V

1. M. Scott Peck, M.D., *The Different Drum* (New York: Touchstone, 1988).

### Part VI

1. Anne W. Schaef quote can be found at http://www.quoteland. com/author/Anne-W-Schaef-Quotes/7683/.

# ABOUT THE AUTHOR

TIM HOEKSTRA IS the mentoring/teaching leader for Suburban Life Community Church, a church he planted more than twenty years ago. Tim and his church community work to learn about and live a life of racial reconciliation and diversity, and are devoted to partnering with under-resourced communities in Chicago. Along with his church work, he also served in past years as a college chaplain and as the associate director of church relations for World Vision Chicago, taking church pastors and leaders to several countries in Africa. He has also served as the coordinator of a running/walking/mentoring program for kids and adults in under-resourced communities on the west side of Chicago for the Steps Foundation. He is currently the coordinator of the Austin Walk/Run Club. He is passionate about seeing churches, ministries, and leaders developed that are ethnically diverse, that honor and submit to those who are impoverished and marginalized, and that seek to unite people across lines of location, socioeconomic position, denomination, and giftedness. Tim has run seven straight Chicago marathons, and in 2009 in celebration of his fiftieth birthday he ran fifty miles, including the Chicago marathon, and raised fifty thousand dollars for clean water wells in Kenya. Tim and Laura, his wife of thirty years, live as a bridge between suburbs and city near the west side of Chicago in River Forest, Illinois, and have three children, two of whom are married. They recently became first-time grandparents.

# CONTACT THE AUTHOR

**WWW.MILESTORUNBEFOREWESLEEP.COM**